PRIMARY SCHOOL

A Parent's Guide

First published in Great Britain in 2010 by
Need2Know
Remus House
Coltsfoot Drive
Peterborough
PE2 9JX
Telephone 01733 898103
Fax 01733 313524
www.need2knowbooks.co.uk

Need2Know is an imprint of Forward Press Ltd.
www.forwardpress.co.uk
SB ISBN 978-1-86144-088-4
Cover photograph: Stockxpert

Contents

Introduction

We all want to do the best for our children and make sure that their school lives are as enjoyable and rewarding as they can be. When your child starts primary school, it can be a scary time as you wonder whether they will make friends and cope academically.

For many parents, the system of primary education seems very different from the one we knew as children. No longer do children automatically attend their local primary school. Instead, parents have to make their way through an often confusing maze of admissions rules. How can you know which school is best for your child and whether they have a chance of getting in? And what's the difference between 'voluntary-controlled' and 'voluntary-aided', anyway?

Schools themselves have changed a lot. Regular inspections by Ofsted, SATs examinations and a single, standardised curriculum have all been introduced in the last 30 years. As a result, some of what your child learns at school – and the way it is learnt – may be confusing and unfamiliar. You will hear teachers using terms like 'Key Stage 1', 'phonics' or 'foundation stage'. Your child will be assessed much more frequently than used to be the case and the school report may rate your child's performance against a set of standardised criteria. When it comes to what is learnt, you will find that the curriculum follows a set pattern, with children in different schools learning about the same topics and, to some extent, using the same materials.

This book provides a guide that will help you choose a school, find your way through the admissions process, understand what your child is learning in school and learn how you can support them. It will take you through all the puzzling acronyms like KS1, SATs and QCDA and explain what they mean, so when a teacher says that your child has achieved a level 4 in literacy, or you read that your school has an Ofsted rating of 2, you will know what it means.

This book will also guide you through the content of the National Curriculum in primary schools, with a clear explanation of what children will cover in the main subject areas. It will advise you about the kinds of activities you can do with

'For many parents, the system of primary education seems very different from the one we knew as children. Instead, parents have to make their way through an often confusing maze of admissions rules.'

your child to help with their schoolwork and guide you to extra resources, so you will know where to go for support if your child is struggling in a particular subject.

By the end of it, you will have a good understanding of how school admissions work, what the National Curriculum is about and how you can help your child get the most out of their time at school.

The rest of the book is divided up into the following chapters:

- Choosing a primary school.
- How admissions work.
- Starting school.
- What your child will learn in school.
- The foundation stage (3-5 years old).
- Key Stage 1 (5-7 years old).
- Key Stage 1 SATs.
- Key Stage 2 (7-11 years old).
- Key Stage 2 SATs.

The best way to read it is from beginning to end, but you may want to dip into the areas that you're most interested in, or refer to it when you need it – when your child is about to take SATs, for example. At the end, you will find recommendations for books and useful web links.

Disclaimer

All the information, dates and website details contained in this book are correct at the time of going to press. Please see the government resources in the help list for the most up-to-date information regarding the admissions process, the National Curriculum and SATs.

Acronyms

DCSF	Department for Children, Schools and Families
DfE	Department for Education (previously DCSF)
EYFS	Early Years Foundation Stage (0-5 years old)
ICT	information and communication technology
ISC	Independent Schools Council
ISI	Independent Schools Inspectorate
KS1	Key Stage 1 (Years 1-2)
KS2	Key Stage 2 (Years 3-6)
LA	local authority
Ofsted	Office of Standards in Education, Children's Services and Skills
PE	physical education
PSHE	personal, social and health education
PTA	Parent Teacher Association
QCDA	Qualifications and Curriculum Development Agency
RE	religious education
SATs	Statutory Assessment Tests
SEF	self-evaluation framework
SENCO	special educational needs co-ordinator
SIP	school improvement plan

Chapter One

Choosing a Primary School

Introduction

The right of parents to specify a preference for a particular primary school was introduced by the 1981 Education Act. Before that, children generally attended their nearest local school. While many parents welcome the opportunity to choose from a range of schools for their child, it has made life a little more complicated; making the right choice for your child can entail wading through masses of information including Ofsted reports, league tables and the school's own prospectus and website.

This chapter explains the different kinds of school available and gives you some suggestions about what you should look for when choosing a school.

Bear in mind that if a school is popular and over-subscribed, it will apply a particular set of admissions criteria to determine which children to accept. Chapter 2 explains how admissions criteria work and what the most common criteria are.

When will my child start school?

In England and Wales, children start school in the academic year that they turn five. The academic year runs from 1st September to 31st August, so if your child was born, for example, between 1st September 2006 and 31st August 2007, they would start school in September 2011. Some schools, however, stagger entry so that younger children start school in the January, rather than the September, of the academic year. In this case, a child born between March and August 2007 would start school in January 2012.

What kinds of schools are available?

Primary, junior and infant schools

Most schools for under-11s are primary schools, teaching both infants (4-7-year-olds) and juniors (7-11-year-olds). Some also have nursery classes aimed at three-year-olds. It can make the transition to school easier for your child if they attend the nursery class first, but this is not compulsory.

There are, however, some schools that only cater for infants and others that only cater for juniors: when your child has finished infant school, they will have to make the transition to junior school. A few local authorities (LAs) run a system of middle schools; in this system, children attend primary school until the age of nine and then attend a middle school between 9-13 years old, before transferring to secondary school.

Whether your child is attending an infant school or a primary school, you need to be aware of the different types of school available.

Community schools

The majority of primary schools in your local area will almost certainly be community schools. They are run by the local authority (LA), which is usually your county council (such as Hertfordshire) or your city council (such as Birmingham). The LA provides the funding and also determines the admissions criteria, which it applies uniformly to all community schools. Community schools all follow the National Curriculum.

Foundation schools

Foundation schools are funded by the LA, but the land and buildings are owned by the school. It is the governing body, rather than the LA, that employs staff and sets admissions rules. Foundation schools make up only about 2% of primary schools in England.

Faith schools

Faith schools are affiliated to a particular religious faith. The overwhelming majority are affiliated either to the Church of England or the Catholic Church, though there are a handful of schools affiliated to other faiths, such as Judaism, Islam, Hinduism or Sikhism. Faith schools follow the National Curriculum, but religious education (RE) lessons tend to focus principally on the faith of the school. The school will also promote the ethos of that faith in other ways – through school assemblies, for example.

There are two kinds of faith schools in the state sector:

- Voluntary-controlled schools – in voluntary-controlled schools, the school land and buildings are owned by a charitable association connected to a religious organisation, e.g. the Church of England. Although church representatives sit on the governing body, the schools are run by the LA, which also decides admissions criteria. These admissions criteria will not necessarily be the same as used for community schools and may give priority to children from the religious group the school is associated with.

- Voluntary-aided schools – as with voluntary-controlled schools, the land and buildings are owned by a charitable association connected to a religious organisation, e.g. the Catholic Church. Voluntary-aided schools have slightly more independence, however, as the school is run by the governing body rather than by the LA. While most of the funding comes from the LA, the charitable association is expected to make a small contribution (10%) to building projects. Admissions rules are decided by the school's governing body and will often give priority to children from the particular religious group that the school is affiliated with. Senior teaching staff may be required to have a particular religious affiliation.

'We wanted a school that was close to home, that we could walk to. But the closest school wasn't available to us, so we visited several schools and eventually chose the local Church of England school; it just felt right when we went to view it.'

Claire, mum of two.

Special schools

Some community schools are designated as special schools. They are tailored to meet the requirements of children with particular sets of special needs, such as severe physical disability or learning difficulties. Although there has been a drive towards inclusion, meaning that some children with special needs are taught in state schools, special schools remain only for children who would find it very difficult to have their needs met in an ordinary school, e.g. children who are deaf or who have severe cerebral palsy.

Provision of special schools is patchy, so if your child does have severe special needs, your options will be fairly limited. If there is no special school tailored to meet your child's particular needs locally, you may have to consider sending your child to a school in a different LA.

Private schools

Private schools, also known as independent or fee-paying schools, are not part of the state system. They are not subject either to LA control or LA admissions rules. They can choose whether or not to enter pupils in Statutory Assessment Tests, usually known as SATs, and many choose not to. Private schools are not obliged to follow the National Curriculum, though the majority do.

Just as state schools vary, so do private schools. Some private schools teach children all the way from age three to age 18, while others stop at age 11. The vast majority offer smaller classes, typically between 10 and 20 pupils, rather than the 30 pupils characteristic of a state school. Some will place a big emphasis on academic achievement, while others are more concerned to provide a nurturing, friendly environment (though of course, it is possible to do both).

Some private schools make a point of offering an alternative to traditional state-based schooling methods, based on a particular educational philosophy, such as Montessori or Steiner. Montessori schools offer a child-centred method of learning, where the child directs their own activity and is guided rather than taught by the teacher. Steiner schools put an emphasis on the development of the 'whole child', and teach a curriculum that requires children to think creatively and imaginatively as well as conceptually.

'What we liked when we first visited the school was that the children were polite and articulate; the cricket pavilion was nice; the playing fields were big and well-kept, and class sizes were good. Above all, though, it was the "feel" of the place – happy and busy and caring.'

Rachel, whose two children go to a private primary school.

The government has plans to set up 'free' schools. These will be small schools set up and run by community groups, charities, teachers or groups of parents. It is unclear at the moment how long it will take to set up a free school, or how many there will eventually be.

How to choose the school

When you choose the school you would like your child to attend, there are lots of things you need to take into account. Before doing anything else, take some time to research admissions rules and find out which schools your child has a realistic chance of getting into. There is no point in applying to a school three miles away if it is heavily over-subscribed and the entire intake comes from within a 500-metre radius of the school.

You can find admissions rules for community schools on your LA's website, and admissions rules for voluntary-controlled and voluntary-aided schools are usually available on the websites of the individual schools. You can also contact the admissions team at your LA or the head of the school to ask if children from your area have been admitted in the past. Independent schools set their own admissions rules – many operate on a 'first come, first served' basis. A few select according to an academic test. You will need to look at the website for each school to find out what the admissions rules are for that school.

When you have a shortlist of schools that look promising, think about the characteristics of the school you'd like your child to attend. Here are some other questions to ask yourself:

- Will my child be happier in a big school or a small school? Is my child shy or outgoing?
- Which school will my child's friends be going to?
- Do I want my child to be able to walk to school?
- Will I need a school that caters for special needs, such as dyslexia?
- Is high academic achievement important to me?
- How important is it that my child is educated in a particular religious faith?

'As a working parent, it made a massive difference to have an after-school club at the school, so it was an extension of play with their friends in a known playground, rather than a new setting and a tiring move at the end of the day.'

Catrin, mum of two.

- Do I need a school that offers wrap-around care (breakfast clubs or after-school clubs) if I need childcare?

- How important is it that my child has access to extra-curricular activities, such as music classes or sports clubs?

There are several ways you can find out more information about what schools are like. Here are some ideas for researching schools in your area.

Website and prospectus

The website and prospectus are a good first port-of-call. They will give you some basic facts about the school, such as how big it is, what clubs it runs and what facilities it offers. The website may also give a link to the school's Ofsted report. However, it's important to remember an impressive website and prospectus are not necessarily indications of a good school, just as a poorly-designed website and prospectus aren't necessarily indications of a bad school. Some schools are simply better at PR and marketing than others.

Other parents

It can be useful to talk to other parents, but you need to take care. Myths about a local school (e.g. 'it has a terrible bullying problem' or 'it's the best school for miles') can establish themselves in a community and hang around for years, long after they have stopped being true. Speaking to parents whose children already attend a school is a better bet. They are more likely to give you a realistic account of what the school is really like, e.g. how good discipline is, how much homework the children get, whether the teaching is engaging or dull and how much help is given to slower learners.

Ofsted or Independent Schools Inspectorate report

Ofsted, which stands for Office for Standards in Education, Children's Services and Skills, is the government body responsible for monitoring the performance of schools in England (but not in Wales, Scotland or Northern Ireland). It was set up in 1992 to replace the system of LA inspections that had been in place up until then.

'I talked to parents, in the park, library or supermarket, whose children had on the school uniform of one of our closest schools and asked them what they thought of it. I went on school visits and looked closely at what the schools had to offer.'

Lynley, mum of one.

It inspects schools approximately every three years, looking at the following criteria:

- The quality of the education provided in the school.
- How far the education provided in the school meets the needs of the range of pupils at the school.
- The educational standards achieved in the school.
- The quality of leadership in, and the management of, the school, including whether the financial resources made available to the school are managed effectively.
- The spiritual, moral, social and cultural development of the pupils at the school.

At the end of the inspection, the inspector or inspectors write a report evaluating the school. Each of the five criteria above has several mini criteria, and the school is given a grade for each one on the following scale:

- 1 = outstanding.
- 2 = good.
- 3 = satisfactory.
- 4 = inadequate.

The school will also be given an overall rating on the same scale. A school that is rated inadequate is sometimes placed on special measures, which means that it needs additional help to improve. Extra funding is made available to the school, and it will receive more support from the LA and frequent re-inspections until it is deemed to have improved.

If a school doesn't link to its Ofsted report from its website, you can find the most recent report on Ofsted's website by searching for the school (see help list). It's worth making a note of when the most recent report was carried out: if it was three years ago, circumstances at the school may have changed – there may be a new head teacher, for example. You could also look at older reports to see if there are any ongoing causes for concern.

If you are considering a private school, then the system is slightly different. If the head teacher is a member of an association affiliated to the Independent Schools Council (ISC), the school will be subject to the ISC's inspection regime, carried out by the Independent Schools Inspectorate (ISI). To find out if the school is a member of ISC, you can use the search facility on the ISC website (www.isc.co.uk). You can see a school's inspection report on the ISI website (see help list) – it will follow a similar format to Ofsted reports, though grades are not awarded for each category.

Private schools that are not subject to the ISI regime are inspected by Ofsted and their reports can be found on the Ofsted website (see help list).

League tables

School league tables, which are published every December, show how well children performed in the Year 6 SATs exams. League tables can be found on the Department for Education (DfE) website (see help list). Each school within an English LA is ranked according to its performance in that summer's SATs. The rankings are determined by the percentage of pupils who achieved level 4 or higher in maths and literacy. Science, which was previously included, has now been dropped from the tests.

A level 4 result represents a standard that the government believes at least 85% of 11-year olds should achieve. As well as ranking schools in order of achievement, the league tables will tell you the percentage of pupils who achieved level 4 in each school.

League tables provide a useful rough guide to academic achievement. However, they need to be approached with caution. Bear in mind:

▪ Results can fluctuate from year to year. Sometimes a school will have an exceptionally talented, or an exceptionally unacademic, intake of Year 6 pupils. It's worth looking at performance over a period of three or four years.

▪ In a small school, poor performance by a handful of children can skew the results. If a school has 30 children in Year 6, for example, three children failing to reach level 4 will mean a drop of 10% in the final score. Absentee children are recorded as having failed to meet the target, so this will be reflected in the score too.

- Some schools are good at 'teaching to the test': coaching pupils to answer the kinds of questions they'll get in the SATs. A good set of results doesn't necessarily mean children are getting a good all-round education.

- Some schools work hard at getting all children up to level 4, while not pushing the more able children. Look at the proportion of children achieving level 5 in the school if you want to have an idea of whether brighter children are being stretched.

- Most importantly, a school's SATs results to a large extent reflect the intake. Schools with a transient population (children continually joining or leaving) will find it hard to achieve a consistent set of good results in Year 6. Schools who take a high proportion of children from very disadvantaged backgrounds, or from non-English speaking homes, or who have special needs, also face a tougher challenge. Looking at the 'value-added' scores can be some help: these rate the school according to the difference between the results achieved in the Year 2 SATs and those achieved in the Year 6 SATs. This is an imperfect measure, however, because a good school will already have made some progress with pupils by the time they reach Year 2. For schools with a highly transient population, the comparison may not be a meaningful one.

You will find more information about SATs in chapters 7 and 9.

Visit the school

This is the single most important thing you can do to help you make your decision – a visit to the school may give you a completely different impression from the one you had beforehand. Some schools will have dedicated slots in which to show prospective parents around; others will allow you to make an individual appointment. Walking around the school gives you a chance to assess things like the quality of work pinned on the walls, how well behaved the children are in class, how motivated the teachers seem, how much space the children have to play in during breaks and how disciplinary problems are dealt with.

If you can, make an appointment to talk to the head teacher after you have been shown around. Have some questions prepared beforehand to get the most out of the meeting. Questions you could ask include:

'The most important thing is to visit all the potential schools and get a feel for the one that you think will suit your child.'

Jayne, mum of two.

- What approach does the school take towards discipline, particularly bullying?

- If a child is behaving badly in class, how will the teacher deal with it?

- How much emphasis does the school place on creative activities, such as dance and music?

- How much homework do children get – and what kind of homework are they asked to do?

- Some schools with a small intake put children of different ages in the same class. If the school does this, what strategy does it have to enable the teacher to cope with two different age groups?

- How does the school cope with children with special needs?

- What is staff turnover like?

- How much time is devoted to teaching maths and literacy? What method is used for teaching children to read?

- Does the school have a 'buddying' system, where older children befriend and watch out for reception children?

- Does the school believe in cross-curricular learning (i.e. using one activity to blend science, maths and literacy skills)?

- Does the school provide foreign language lessons?

- What extension activities does it have for more able children?

- How many children join and leave the school each year (outside the normal reception intake and Year 6 departures)?

- Does the school have a home-school agreement? (A home-school agreement is a contract between the school and the parent, in which both the school and the parent make certain commitments. The school might commit to providing regular homework, for example, while the parent commits to making sure homework is completed on time.)

- You could also ask to see copies of the school's policies on particular areas, such as behaviour, literacy, equal opportunities or special needs.

'We looked at the quality of resources and displays, and blacklisted one school because it had spelling mistakes and misplaced apostrophes in the reception class display.'

Catrin, mum of two.

Armed with all this information and research, you should be ready to make a decision on your preferred schools and begin applying for a school place. Chapter 2 explains more about how the admissions process works.

Summing Up

- Your child will start school in the academic year they turn five.

- Most schools in the state sector are known as community schools, but there are also schools known as voluntary-aided or voluntary-controlled schools which are affiliated to a religious body.

- You can find out information about your local schools by looking at the school websites, reading the school prospectuses, looking at Ofsted reports, talking to other parents and looking at league tables.

- The best way of getting a feel for a school and deciding whether it is right for your child is to pay a visit – try to arrange a time to talk to the head teacher too.

Chapter Two

How Admissions Work

Introduction

In this chapter, we look at the tangled subject of school admissions. Because admissions policies vary from LA to LA, and even (in the case of faith schools) from school to school, they can be quite complicated to untangle. This chapter looks at the most common criteria for admissions rules and how to maximise the chances of getting your child into your preferred school.

We also look at what to do if your child doesn't get into your chosen school, how to make an appeal and how to find an alternative school if the appeal doesn't succeed.

Why do we need school admissions rules?

Before the 1981 Education Act, LAs had control over where children went to school, and generally they made sure that children attended their nearest school. If the school didn't have enough places, some children (perhaps those newest to the area) were allocated places at a school further away.

The 1981 Act gave parents the legal right to express a preference about which school their child should attend, but although we often talk about parental choice, nobody is guaranteed a place at their preferred school. If you prefer the look of a school five kilometres away to your local school, then you have the right to apply for a place there. The problem arises when lots of other people decide they prefer that school too, so there has to be a system for allocating the places. These are known as the admissions rules.

Class sizes

There's another important piece of legislation you need to know about. In 1998, the government introduced a law that said that an infant class (i.e. a reception class, a Year 1 class or a Year 2 class) should not have more than 30 pupils. This was in response to concerns that some classes were just too big, with 35 or more children.

The downside of the legislation has been that schools have to enforce class sizes rigorously. So if 31 children want to attend a school and it only has one class of 30, one child will have to attend another school. Before 1998, schools could sometimes be a bit more flexible. It also makes it more difficult for parents to win appeals if their child doesn't get into their preferred school.

Who decides the admissions rules?

In most cases, the rules are determined by the LA and apply equally to all the community schools in their area.

In the case of voluntary-controlled schools (i.e. schools with a religious affiliation), the admissions rules are agreed between the LA and the school governing body. They may differ from the rules used for the community schools and may give preference to children whose parents practise the religious faith of that school.

In the case of voluntary-aided schools (i.e. schools with a religious affiliation), the rules are determined by the school governing body and will usually give priority to children from the same religious faith as the school. The school may require you to fill in a separate application form as well as the LA form and the closing date for applications may also be earlier than the LA date.

The government's School Admissions Code (see book list) outlines a framework for admissions for all LAs in England. It also applies to schools in cases where the school is responsible for admissions. Some of it is mandatory (that is, LAs and schools are legally obliged to follow it), while some is advisory (LAs and schools are expected to follow it, but it is not legally enforced). For example, the Code states that interviews, either with parents or children, must not form part of the admissions process, which is a legal obligation.

How do they work?

Each LA draws up its admissions rules by taking into account the particular requirements of the local area. It isn't always easy to devise a set of rules that satisfactorily meet the needs of all parents and children in the area.

Imagine, for example, that the LA allocates places at all schools to children who live nearest the school. This may work well in urban areas, where most people live within a couple of kilometres of a school. But if you are living in a rural part of the LA and your nearest school is 10 kilometres away, all the places will have been allocated to local children, so there's a good chance that your child will, instead, be allocated a place at another school 20 kilometres away. The LA has to adjust for this in its rules.

Often rules will change slightly from year to year to adjust for population changes, or to correct perceived unfairnesses caused by the previous year's rules. It's important to keep an eye on rule changes, which are available on your LA's website, because they could affect your child's ability to get a place. The fact that children in your street have always been given places at a particular school is no guarantee that your child will be offered a place there.

What are the admissions rules criteria?

LAs will usually come up with a list of about half-a-dozen criteria for admitting children. These will then be applied in sequence until the full quota for a school has been reached. It may be that if a lot of children are admitted under the first few rules, there will be no places left for children who may qualify under the rules lower down the list.

Rules for community schools usually include the following:

- Whether the child has a Statement of Special Educational Needs that requires them to go to a particular school.

- Whether the child or the family has a medical or social requirement to go to a particular school.

- Whether the child has siblings at the school.

- How near the child lives to the school.

■ Whether the school is the nearest for that child.

An example

This is what a typical set of admissions rules for a community primary school in an LA might be:

1. Children with a Statement of Special Educational Needs requiring them to go to a particular school are given priority. Explanation: all the children who apply under rule 1 must be offered a place by law.

2. Looked after children (children in care) are given next priority as a government requirement.

3. Children with a medical or social need to go to the school. Explanation: for example, a medical need might be that your child is a wheelchair user and needs to go to a school adapted for wheelchair use. A social need might be that your child suffers from crippling shyness and needs to be with existing friends. If you want your child to be awarded a place under this rule, then you will need to supply a supporting statement from a doctor or a psychologist. Your application will then be considered by a panel of officers at the LA.

4. Children with a sibling at the school. Explanation: most (but by no means all) LAs have a sibling rule so that parents don't have to travel to separate schools. If a sibling rule is in place, it is likely to specify that the sibling will still be at the school when the second child starts school. If your elder child is currently in Year 6 and about to start secondary school, your younger child won't get a place under this rule. Different LAs will have different definitions of sibling, but they will usually specify that the children should live in the same house. If your child lives with you, but their older half-sister lives with your ex-partner, then your child will not qualify under this rule.

5. Children for whom this is their nearest school. Explanation: this means that if the school is your nearest school, your child will have priority over children who may live nearer but have another school even nearer them. For example, suppose Mr and Mrs Smith want their child to go to Treetops school, three kilometres away, and it is their nearest school. Mr and Mrs Jones also want their child to go to Treetops. They live one kilometre from

Treetops school, but are only half a kilometre from Green Meadow school. Mr and Mrs Smith's child will have priority over Mr and Mrs Jones' child when it comes to deciding who gets offered a place at Treetops.

6. Children who live nearest the school. Explanation: of the children who didn't qualify under rules 1-5, places will be offered to those who live nearest.

These rules are just hypothetical, of course; admissions rules differ from LA to LA, though all LAs will have a rule that automatically offers places to children with a Statement of Special Educational Needs that requires them to go to a particular school.

Some authorities have a catchment rule, giving priority to children within a particular catchment area – though they are not allowed to guarantee places for children in a catchment.

A few authorities don't have a sibling rule. It's worth bearing this in mind if you have a younger child but are planning on moving further away from the school before the child reaches school age.

If your child has a medical or social problem that might require them to go to a particular school, you should mention this on the form (and get a supporting statement) – but it is by no means a guarantee that a place will be offered.

Voluntary-aided and voluntary-controlled schools

Voluntary-aided and voluntary-controlled schools are more usually known as faith schools or church schools. Each voluntary-aided or voluntary-controlled school will have its own rules, which will usually be different from the rules that apply to community schools. They may admit some children under sibling or geographical rules, but they will also hold some places for children of the school's particular religious denomination. If you are applying under the religious denomination rule, you may be expected to supply either a baptism certificate or an accompanying letter from the priest, vicar or other religious leader to confirm your religious affiliation.

For voluntary-aided schools, you will need to submit a separate application to the school as well as the one you submit to the LA.

Can I apply for a school in a different LA?

You can apply for a school in an LA even if you don't live there. This is particularly common in London, where many people live on or near the borders of different London boroughs. If you do this, you will need to contact the relevant LA and fill in a separate application form. Bear in mind that this LA may have different admissions rules.

How do I apply?

Most LAs will allow you to apply for three schools, listed in order of preference. Use your preferences wisely! It makes sense to include at least one school that you have a strong chance of being accepted for. Many parents have found themselves being offered a school that they don't want (usually the nearest school with places available) because they weren't accepted for any of their three choices.

Be aware that the order in which you put the schools will not normally affect your chances of being offered a place in a particular school. The reason for listing them in order of preference is so the LA can offer you, if possible, your preferred school.

You will automatically be sent a paper form to fill in, which will have to be returned to the LA by a particular date. Many LAs also give you the option to apply online.

There will be a booklet sent with the form listing the LA schools you can apply for and giving information about the number of children admitted to each school. The booklet will explain the admissions rules for community schools and the different rules for the voluntary-aided and voluntary-controlled schools.

When you fill the form in, you will have to give your child's name and date of birth, together with details of whether they have any siblings at the schools you are applying to, whether there is a statement of special needs, and whether there are any particular social or medical requirements that mean it is preferable for your child to attend your first choice of school.

If you have problems filling the form in, you can call the admissions team at your LA to ask for help.

If you require a supporting statement from your GP or religious leader, you should make an appointment to see them and ask for it. Although they will be used to receiving these requests, it is still worth asking for it in good time. A few weeks before the closing date is recommended.

Obtaining a Statement of Special Educational Needs can be a long and laborious process. If your child already attends nursery or pre-school, you should begin by talking to the person responsible in that setting for special educational needs. This person is known as the special educational needs co-ordinator (SENCO) and will help assess whether your child has special needs and, if so, what special needs they have. If necessary, the SENCO can contact the LA to ask for a statutory assessment. If your child doesn't attend a nursery or pre-school, you can do this yourself.

The LA has to let you know within six weeks whether they will carry out the assessment. If they agree, it may then take several more weeks before they begin the assessment, and, having carried out the assessment, they may not agree that your child needs a statement. Government rules state that the whole process from beginning to end should not take more than 26 weeks.

The LA is unlikely to send you a reminder to fill in the form, so make sure you return it by the closing date. If you forget to do so, you will be allocated a school that has not filled its places, though you will be able to go on the waiting list for your preferred school.

When do I put in my application?

You will normally apply for a school place the autumn before your child is due to start school. So if your child is due to start school in September 2012 or January 2013, you will need to submit your application in autumn 2011.

What if I have twins or triplets?

The School Admissions Code says that admissions criteria should allow twins and triplets to be kept together in the same school. It then adds, 'as long as they comply with the Education (Infant Class Sizes) (England) Regulations'.

That does mean, unfortunately, that if there is only one place left in a school and the next children on the list are twins, then they may be offered places in separate schools. It is rare, but it does happen.

How do I complain about admissions rules?

LAs carry out a consultation every year about their admissions rules. As a parent of a prospective school-age child, you have the right to make your views about the admissions rules known. Unfortunately, many parents don't realise they are unhappy with the admissions rules until their child has failed to get into their preferred school. It is worth taking time to read the proposed admissions rules beforehand and make your views known to the LA.

You have two other options:

■ If your child fails to win a place at your preferred school, you can appeal against the decision.

■ If you think the admissions rules are unfair, you can take your concerns to the Office of the School Adjudicator. You don't have to wait until your child has been refused a place to do this.

What if my child isn't offered a place at my preferred school?

If your child is allocated a school that you're not happy with, you can put your child's name on the waiting list for your preferred school or schools. LAs will usually allow you to go on the waiting list for more than one school. In some schools, it is quite common for children to drop out before they start school, so you may still have a good chance of getting your child into the school you want.

You can ask your LA to tell you where your child is on the waiting list, though this information may not be available immediately. You can also ask to see the criteria by which other children were admitted. For example, the LA may be able to tell you that the last child admitted lived 1,200m away from the school; if you live 1,250m away, you know that you stand a better chance of getting in on the waiting list than if you live 2,000m away.

How do I appeal against a decision?

If your child isn't allocated your first choice of school, the LA will automatically send you a leaflet explaining how you can appeal. You will have to fill in a form outlining the grounds for appeal, and a few weeks later attend a panel interview where between three and five independent adjudicators will ask you your reasons for appealing.

Because of the limit on class sizes, it's not easy to win a primary school appeal. If the primary school you want your child to attend has already filled its quota of places, there are only three grounds for appeal:

- Your child would have been offered a place if the admission arrangements had been properly implemented: this means that the LA or school made an error when applying its own admissions rules. This is fairly unusual.

- A place would have been offered if the arrangements had not been contrary to criteria set out in the School Admissions Code: the LA or school may have broken the School Admissions Code, e.g. by conducting interviews of parents or asking for a financial contribution to the school.

- The decision to refuse admission was not one which a reasonable admission authority would have made in the circumstances of the case. In the School Admission Appeals Code, this is defined as 'a decision which is so outrageous in its defiance of logic or of accepted moral standards that no sensible person who had applied his mind to the question could have arrived at it.' As you can imagine, it is very difficult indeed to win an appeal on these grounds, because it implies that the admissions body has rejected the application on entirely arbitrary grounds.

Despite this, parents do win primary school appeals; published figures show that in 2008, 22,220 appeals were made for primary school places, and 6,190 were decided in favour of the parents. It's difficult to explain this anomaly, but

'The appeal process was quite straightforward, but in reality, we knew that we had little chance of success. However, we felt that we had to go through with it so that we could be confident that we had left no stone unturned'.

Jonathan, dad of two.

it suggests either that LAs are being very lax in the administration of their own rules, or that some appeals panels are interpreting the rules in a fairly flexible manner.

To improve your chances of winning an appeal, you may want to consult an education lawyer. There are also organisations that offer advice, such as School Appeals and the Advisory Centre for Education, a charity offering free advice on educational matters (see help list).

Office of the Schools Adjudicator

If you are unhappy with the admission arrangements in your LA, you can take your concerns to the Office of the Schools Adjudicator, a body set up by the government to adjudicate in disputes about admissions. The schools adjudicators will not look at cases involving individual children, just at whether the admissions rules themselves are fair.

The schools adjudicators can:

- Adjudicate on objections to admission arrangements. So if you think a particular admissions rule is unfair, the adjudicators can look into it and make a decision.

- Decide on requests to vary determined admission arrangements. In these cases, an LA may have finalised admissions arrangements, and then decided it wants to change them, perhaps because of exceptional circumstances such as the closure of a school. It can only change the rules with the agreement of the adjudicator.

- Determine appeals from schools against a direction from the LA to admit a particular pupil. If a child has been excluded from other schools, or has moved into the area in the middle of the school year, the LA may direct a school to provide a place for that child. The school can appeal against this direction to the adjudicator.

The adjudicator's decision is binding, so if the adjudicator tells the LA to change the rules, the LA must comply.

Summing Up

- Admissions rules are determined by the LA, except in the case of voluntary-aided schools, where they are determined by the governing body.

- Admissions rules use a set of criteria to give priority to particular children.

- The criteria will always give priority to children with a Statement of Special Educational Needs that names a particular school.

- Other criteria are likely to include whether the child has particular medical or social needs, whether they have a sibling at the school and how far they live from the school.

- If your child fails to get into your preferred school, you can go on the waiting list for the school you want and, if you feel you have a strong case, make an appeal against the decision.

- If you are unhappy with admissions arrangements in your LA, you can take your case to the Office of the Schools Adjudicator.

- For specific information on special educational needs, see *Special Educational Needs - A Parent's Guide* (Need2Know).

Chapter Three

Starting School

Starting primary school is a major life event for parents as well as for children. Children of four or five can still feel like our babies, so waving goodbye on that first day can be hard for both parties. In this chapter, there are some tips on how to make that process a little easier, both for you and your child.

For your child...

Get to know other children

If you know other children due to start at the same school, it's worth trying to arrange a get-together for the children before they start. It helps to see a familiar face on the first day.

Most primary schools have a settling-in morning for new children at the end of the term before they are due to start. The school will let you know in advance when it is due to take place. Do make sure, if you can, that your child attends the settling-in morning, as it's a good opportunity to familiarise themselves with the setting and even to meet new friends. If your child already attends the school nursery, then this gives them a head start as the environment will already be familiar.

Learn some basic skills

Once children start school, they should be able to manage things like getting dressed and undressed for PE, going to the toilet by themselves and wiping their own nose. If your child will be having school dinners, make sure they know how to use a knife and fork correctly.

Practise paying attention

It will help your child a lot if they know how to sit still and listen to what the teacher is saying. Do your best to encourage listening skills in your child, and practise doing activities that require concentration, like building a model out of Lego or doing a jigsaw. Playing games like Snakes and Ladders is a good way of teaching your child social skills such as taking turns.

Learn to ask for help

Your child needs to know where to turn to help if something goes wrong – for example, if your child can't do shoelaces up, or if another child is being mean to them. Let your child know that they should ask the teacher for help, and that if there are any problems they can't tell the teacher, they should tell you.

Make preparing for school fun

If the school has requirements for particular pieces of equipment, you can buy them together, so your child can have the fun of choosing their own pencil case, water bottle or lunchbox.

Read some books

There are some lovely books about starting primary school that might help reassure your child if they're nervous:

- *Starting School* by Alan and Janet Ahlberg (Puffin Books, 1990).
- *I am Too Absolutely Small for School* by Lauren Child (Orchard Books, 2010).
- *Topsy and Tim Start School* by Jean and Gareth Adamson (Ladybird Books, 2009).
- *Kevin Goes to School* by Liesbet Siegers (Frances Lincoln, 2005).

'We spent a summer getting him to practise wiping his own bottom and flushing, getting him to pick out his things from a pile of miscellaneous items and work out where to keep them safely, making sure he could dress himself and getting him to put stuff away, such as pencils into a pencil case.'

Catrin, mum of two.

For you...

Buy the uniform

Make sure that you have a complete uniform list and that you buy the uniform well in advance. The school will provide you with a uniform list beforehand, and the list will usually be available on the school website and in the school prospectus too. Schools may sell some items of uniform (such as those containing the school logo) themselves, or they may refer you to a local shop. Bear in mind that children get dirty very quickly, so you'll need several items of things like white tops and sweatshirts. It can be a good idea to buy skirts or trousers with elasticated waists, to make it easier for children to get changed themselves. You'll also need to buy PE kit, and some schools require children to wear plimsolls indoors.

If the uniform is expensive, ask the school if it is planning a sale of second-hand uniforms – many schools do.

Know the starting and finishing times

Make sure you know when school starts. Schools often have different starting and finishing times for new reception children from the rest of the school – they may start a day later, or they may do mornings only for the first week. It's not unknown for parents to turn up a day early or pick up too late. The school will provide you with all of this information before your child is due to start.

Avoid pressure

Most children get fed up very quickly with adults saying, 'Are you looking forward to starting school?' or 'Isn't it exciting that you'll be starting school soon?' While it's tempting to talk up how wonderful school is going to be, it's not a good idea to overdo it. They'll almost certainly be apprehensive about it, and you need to give your child time to talk about any worries they have. On the other hand, try not to frighten your child with comments like, 'The teacher will be cross if you behave like that in school'.

Don't dismiss their fears

If your child is anxious about starting school, listen carefully to their concerns and answer them as best you can. Even if it seems silly to you, the concerns may seem like a big thing to your child. They may be worried about things that you hadn't even thought about, like how they'll find the toilet, whether they'll like school dinners or how long they have to stay in school each day. Reassure your child that it will be all the other children's first day at a new school as well, and at the end of the school day, you or a carer will be there to pick them up.

Make the most of the first day

If you don't have to go to work after dropping your child off at school, one mum suggests turning the day into a ceremony for you too – perhaps by meeting friends somewhere for coffee and cake.

Be prepared for primary school blues

Children can take a while to settle into primary school. Once the initial excitement has worn off, the days can seem long and some children get tired – mentally if not physically. Some ideas to help you with this phase could be:

- Having a snack ready for when you pick your child up at the end of the day – it can give a bit of a lift to a grumpy child.

- Letting your child burn off some energy for a while at the end of the day – it is likely they will have a good deal of pent-up energy after sitting down all day.

- Trying not to overdo the out-of-school activities in the early days. It can all get too much.

- Trying not to expect your child to tell you lots about what's happening in school, particularly not when you pick them up. Responses such as 'Mmm', 'Don't know' and 'Can't remember' are common. Children are sometimes more willing to chat about what they've been doing when you're tucking them up in bed.

'Kieran was determined not to go to school. Eventually, I took him into school and bought him a school hat. He was very scathing of the whole idea but brightened up when the reception teacher let him have a peek into the classroom. There were toys in it. School was OK after that.'

Kerry, mum of three.

School governors and the PTA

If you don't know any other parents at your child's school, the first few weeks can be lonely for you too. Some parents complain about feeling excluded by cliques on the playground. Of course, 'clique' can just be another word for a group of friends who already know each other. The easiest way to deal with this is simply to go up to another parent on the playground and start talking – there's every chance that they are feeling isolated too.

Not everyone is a joiner or a committee person, but if you do want to get more involved in your child's school and you have the time, then joining the parent teacher association (PTA) or becoming a parent governor are both good ways of finding out more about the school and joining in with school life.

The school secretary will be able to give you contact names for the PTA, but there's every likelihood that the information will be posted on the school's website or in the school newsletter. Vacancies for parent governors will usually be advertised in the school newsletter, and if there is more than one candidate for a position, you will have to stand for election by the parent body.

Being involved in the PTA can take up a few hours a term or a few hours a week, depending on the responsibilities you take on. You may just be required to man a stall at the summer fete or take tickets at the school disco, or you may find yourself in charge of organising all the fundraising events – it's up to you.

School governing bodies usually have one full meeting a term, lasting about two or three hours. You may also sit on one or more sub-committees (such as personnel or health and safety), which also meet termly. If you take on more responsibility, such as chairing one of the committees, you will probably find that your duties take up more of your time (particularly if you are involved in recruiting staff, for example), but being a school governor does not have to be a time-consuming job.

Becoming a governor helps you learn more about how school works and gives you the opportunity to influence decisions, such as the hiring of staff, or policies on uniform. Some schools also welcome parents who are able to help out during school hours e.g. listening to pupils read.

Summing Up

- You can help your child prepare for school by introducing them to children who will be in the same class, making sure they have basic skills like being able to dress themselves and making the process of getting ready for school fun.

- Make sure you are well-prepared for the first day by having the uniform ready, and other accessories such as lunchboxes and plimsolls.

- Don't underestimate your child's anxiety, and try to answer any questions honestly and reassuringly.

- Getting involved in school life, for example by joining the PTA, can make you feel more integrated into the school.

Chapter Four

What Your Child Will Learn at School

Introduction

All state schools in England teach the National Curriculum. This chapter will give you an overview of what's in the National Curriculum and how it's taught. It will explain how your child will be assessed and how the school will report on your child's progress.

This chapter also explains the part played by bodies such as the Qualifications and Curriculum Development Agency (QCDA) and Ofsted in determining how the National Curriculum is taught.

What is the National Curriculum?

Before the National Curriculum, which was introduced as part of the Education Reform Act in 1988, schools were free, within reason, to teach what they wanted, the way they wanted. That all changed. These days, the school day is largely filled with activities prescribed by the National Curriculum.

The National Curriculum sets out in detail:

- The subjects each school must teach.

- What skills, knowledge and understanding children should have at each age.

- A set of targets that children should attain at particular stages.

■ A framework for assessing and reporting progress.

Why have a National Curriculum?

With a National Curriculum in place, the government can be sure that every state school is teaching the same thing to its pupils. This offers certain advantages for government, teachers and parents:

■ It makes it easier to measure how successful schools are in teaching children what they need to know.

■ Children can be tested on what they've learnt, giving parents useful information about their child's progress and making it easier to compare schools' performance.

■ Government agencies and private organisations can create teaching and learning resources, such as books, websites and DVDs, that can be used by all schools.

■ Parents can find out what their children will be learning and help them.

■ Teachers can move from school to school knowing that they will be teaching the same curriculum.

What are the objections to a National Curriculum?

The National Curriculum has been controversial since its inception. Here are some of the problems:

■ Deciding what should be included in a National Curriculum, and what should be left out, isn't easy. The contents have been changed many times since 1988 – and may change again soon as a result of the change of government. Many teachers have complained about the burden of constantly having to meet new requirements.

■ Critics of the National Curriculum have attacked it for being too narrow and too prescriptive, emphasising maths and literacy at the expense of creative subjects such as music and art. It allows little freedom for schools, let alone individual teachers, to make their own decisions about what children should learn, or how they should learn it.

- Some people feel that the idea of central government deciding what children should learn offers too many opportunities for ideological control of the curriculum, particularly in politically-charged subjects such as history or citizenship.

- Because the National Curriculum goes hand-in-hand with SATs, many people feel there is a danger that schools will teach children how to pass the tests rather than help them learn, and that children remain under constant pressure to achieve academically.

The key stages

When your child is at primary school, you'll often hear the following terms: foundation stage, Key Stage 1 (KS1) and Key Stage 2 (KS2). These stages refer to particular age groups.

- Foundation stage refers to the nursery and reception years – children aged 3-5 years old. Early Years Foundation Stage (EYFS) is also used and, strictly speaking, refers to children aged 0-5.

- KS1 covers Years 1 and 2 at primary school (children aged 5-7).

- KS2 covers Year 3 up to Year 6 (children aged 7-11).

At secondary school, your child will go through two more key stages:

- KS3 covers Year 7 to Year 9 (children aged 11-14).

- KS4 covers Year 9 to Year 11 (children aged 14-16).

Subjects in the primary curriculum

The following subjects are compulsory for all primary school children aged 5-11, during KS1 and KS2.

- Literacy (sometimes referred to as 'English').

- Maths.

- Science.

- Design and technology.

- Information and communication technology (ICT).

- History.

- Geography.

- Art and design.

- Music.

- Physical education (PE).

Literacy, maths and science are known as core subjects. The other subjects are known as foundation subjects.

Schools also have to teach RE, although parents can choose to withdraw their children from RE lessons. RE is taught according to a locally agreed syllabus, and is expected to reflect the fact that the religious traditions in Great Britain are in the main Christian, while taking account of the teachings and practices of the other principal religions represented in Great Britain. Faith schools are exempt from the locally-agreed syllabus and can create their own RE syllabus.

Currently, personal, social and health education (PSHE) is an optional subject in primary schools. Plans to make it statutory from 2011 are now unlikely to go ahead.

You can find out more about what is taught within the core subjects in chapters 6 and 8.

Knowledge, skills and understanding

Each subject in the National Curriculum is divided into eight levels that will be covered between the ages of five and 16. So a five- or six-year-old will usually be working within level 1, and a 14-year-old will be working within level 6 or 7. For each level, the National Curriculum lists:

- What each child should know.

- What skills each child should have.

- What each child should understand.

For example, literacy is divided into three components:

- Speaking and listening.

- Reading.

- Writing.

The National Curriculum describes what children who have achieved level 1 in writing are able to do:

> 'Pupils' writing communicates meaning through simple words and phrases. In their reading or their writing, pupils begin to show awareness of how full stops are used. Letters are usually clearly shaped and correctly orientated.'

There is more detail about what your child will learn at each level in chapters 6 and 8.

How subjects are taught

The National Curriculum puts a lot of emphasis on literacy and maths – to the extent that it requires children to spend at least an hour each on literacy and maths every day. The content of the literacy and maths curricula is specified to a fine level of detail.

Because science is a core subject, there must also be two lessons of science a week. Time allocated to other subjects may vary – the school may decide to do history one term and geography the next, for example, or it might teach both subjects in each term.

In most schools, you'll find that children sit around tables, with five or six children per table. Some teachers prefer to arrange them in ability groups, either all of the time or just for specific subjects, but this won't necessarily be the case. Most classes will now have a teaching assistant as well as a teacher, who will help with activities such as listening to the children reading.

Teachers typically use a mix of approaches when teaching a subject such as maths or literacy. They'll often begin with a whole class session, where the teacher stands at the front – usually these days with an interactive whiteboard rather than an old-fashioned blackboard or whiteboard.

An interactive whiteboard looks similar to an ordinary whiteboard, but it's connected to a computer. A projector projects whatever's on the computer screen onto the board. The clever bit is that the teacher – or pupils – can interact with the computer by touching the screen with a finger or a special pen. So if the interactive whiteboard is displaying a sum, a pupil can write the answer onto the screen and the whole class can see immediately if it is correct or not.

Once the whole class session is complete, children will usually be given work to do at their tables. Then there'll be another whole-class session to finish off.

Not all lessons will work like this, of course – sometimes children will be working individually, in pairs or in groups. Increasingly, you'll find children using computers across the curriculum in subjects such as history, geography and maths. Although some schools still have ICT suites where children can use computers, the trend now is for schools to buy laptop computers that children can use in their normal classroom.

Attainment targets in each subject

Your child's progress in the main National Curriculum subjects (literacy, maths and science) will be measured in a series of levels that go from one to eight. At certain ages children are expected to have reached a particular level:

- At age seven, children are expected to have reached level 2.
- At age 11, they are expected to have reached level 4.

The majority of children (about 80% nationally) will reach these levels, and some will reach a higher level. Here are the KS2 results in England for 2009:

	Pupils reaching level 4	Pupils reaching level 5
Literacy	80%	29%
Maths	79%	35%

Please note, percentages in the table don't add up to 100 because children reaching level 5 will also have reached level 4.

(Source: *National Curriculum Assessments at Key Stage 2 in England 2009*, DfE.)

To make it a little bit more complicated but much more precise, each level is divided into sub-levels 'a', 'b' and 'c', where 'a' is the highest level of achievement – e.g. a score of 2a is better than a score of 2c.

Assessing and reporting progress

Teachers keep a record of each child's progress against attainment targets both in the core subjects of literacy, maths and science and in the foundation subjects (geography, history, ICT and so on).

When you receive written progress reports from the school, or when you attend a consultation with your child's teacher, the teacher will be able to tell you how your child is doing in terms of meeting those targets. For example, maths has an attainment target called 'Number and algebra'. Level 1 for that target specifies: 'Pupils count, order, add and subtract numbers when solving problems involving up to 10 objects. They read and write the numbers involved.'

Your teacher will use that information to assign a level to your child's performance in the core subjects, which will give you an idea of how their performance compares with the expected attainment for that age group.

Schools generally offer two consultations with parents (also known as parents' evenings) a year, in the autumn and spring terms. You will be sent a letter a week or so in advance letting you know when the consultation is. The teacher will tell you how your child is progressing against targets, and how your child is

'My husband was totally confused when presented on the first parents' evening by a Venn diagram type affair which was supposed to represent our daughter – and he's got a PhD in computational modelling.'

Hannah, mum of two.

coping socially, e.g. whether they pay attention in class and whether they have made friends. Normally, you will be allocated only 10 or 15 minutes with the teacher, so prepare well.

Academic Janine Spencer, quoted in *The Times'* SchoolGate blog, offers the following tips for parents' evenings:

- Prepare a list of questions.
- Know what you would like to take away from the discussion.
- Talk to your child beforehand to find out if they have any concerns about school.
- Be prepared for positive and negative comments.
- Request next steps from the teacher.

If you don't understand what the teacher is talking about, ask for a clearer explanation – teachers can forget that not everybody is familiar with educational jargon.

Remember, too, that if you aren't happy with the outcome of the consultation, you can ask for another meeting with the teacher after school.

School reports

At the end of the year, your child will receive a school report. If you're old enough, you may remember reports that said things like 'Could try harder' or 'Weak in mathematics'. These days, reports can be difficult to interpret because they tend to use the terminology of National Curriculum targets, and they almost certainly won't tell you how your child is doing compared with other children in the class. For example, you'll be unlikely to discover that your child is top of the class in literacy.

One mum, Linda, was baffled when the entry for maths in her daughter's school report read:

'It's important to be clear what you want to get out of parents' evenings. I work out whether there are bits I need to bring up beforehand. I take notes for when I want to feed back to the children. But if there is an issue, arranging a separate meeting is a better policy.'

Catrin, mum of two.

Need2Know

> 'Melissa is beginning to try different approaches and to find ways of overcoming difficulties that arise when she is solving problems. She discusses her work using mathematical language and represents it using symbols and simple diagrams. She is beginning to discuss her mathematical work and is beginning to explain her thinking.'

As Linda says, 'What else would she be doing in maths, exactly? The focus is on what the children have done, not how they've got on, where they need help or have excelled, or even what they've enjoyed.'

If you're unhappy with this approach, the best thing to do is to talk to the teacher about it to try to gain a clearer idea of how your child is performing.

Homework

Most primary schools now give homework to children, even the very youngest. When your child is in reception class, the homework might just be a reading book. When they're older, expect your child to have a list of spellings to learn each week, and perhaps some written homework as well.

As children progress through primary school, they're likely to be given homework that will require them to find out information on the Internet. If you have a computer your child can use, try to keep it an open area where you can see what your child is doing – it's better not to put it in your child's bedroom. If necessary, install parental controls software to protect your child from some of the more harmful content on the Internet. For more information about how to protect your child, see www.thinkuknow.co.uk.

Homework can be a source of stress for both parents and children. Some teachers have a tendency to set homework that can only be carried out with the help of parents – which perhaps defeats the point. Others may simply give out sheets of sums or literacy exercises related to the work that's been done in class.

'My son is in Year 1 and has a book to read with me which changes three times a week – we have to spend 15 minutes each day reading.'

Claire, mum of two.

Because homework can be such a contentious issue, the best approach is to set aside a certain amount of time each week (perhaps half an hour or an hour) in which your child does homework. If it isn't finished by the end of that half hour, then leave it – don't expect your child to spend hours struggling. If the teacher is unhappy with this approach, then talk it through with the school, but there is little point in forcing your child to devoting masses of time to homework for the sake of it.

Provide help if your child asks for it, but avoid doing the homework for them. If something needs looking up on the Internet, for example, show them how to search for the information themselves.

'I've had a range of incomprehensible school reports, such as "K can chase after the ball and stop it", meaning she can't catch yet but she runs in the right direction. I'm now getting better at reading between the lines.'

Catrin, mum of two.

How do I know the school is teaching the National Curriculum correctly?

Schools' activities are tightly controlled these days, with lots of external bodies telling them what they should be doing and making sure they're doing it. Here are a few of the relevant organisations:

■ QCDA – the QCDA is a government organisation, which used to be called the QCA. Its job is to decide the content for the National Curriculum and to create the SATs to measure children's progress. It consults with teachers and head teachers, as well as other people involved in education, to make sure it keeps up with current good practice and expert thinking.

■ Ofsted – although school inspectors have been around since the 19th century, Ofsted as a body was created and given wide-ranging powers in 1993. Ofsted is also a government body, and it's responsible for carrying out regular inspections of schools to make sure they are teaching the curriculum effectively and meeting the needs of pupils and parents. It operates within a closely defined set of criteria. Ofsted has no remit in Northern Ireland, Scotland or Wales, but similar roles are carried out by the Education Inspectorate, Her Majesty's Inspectorate of Education and Estyn respectively.

■ LAs – LAs have responsibility for state schools in their particular area, which may be a county, a city or a borough. LAs provide each school with a budget, which the school then manages individually. Some services, such as special needs provision, are managed by the LA and bought in by schools.

You may have heard LAs referred to as local education authorities or LEAs, but these terms are no longer in use. This is because these days LAs have departments dealing with children's services, which have responsibility both for education and for children's social services.

Schools are given a lot of encouragement to monitor and report on their own progress:

- All schools have to fill in a self-evaluation form (SEF) to record their strengths and weaknesses. Ofsted then uses this form as a basis for its inspection. The forms can be a useful way of encouraging schools to think about what they do well, what they do badly and how they need to improve.

- All schools have to create and maintain a school improvement plan (SIP), which performs a similar role to the SEF. The plan sets out the areas where the school thinks it's doing well, the areas it needs to improve, and how it plans to do it. This might include sending teachers on training courses, for example, introducing ICT into the classroom or making homework more focused on particular curriculum areas.

- Each school also has a school improvement partner – an LA employee who works with the school to review its SIP, help it set new targets and priorities, and let the school know what resources are available to help it meet those targets.

The Rose Report

Since 2003, the last government had been trying to make the National Curriculum for primary schools less prescriptive, and to encourage teachers to move away from teaching specific subjects to teaching topics. For example, instead of teaching history, you could teach a topic such as chocolate with an approach from a history perspective (when chocolate was first introduced into Europe; the role of chocolate manufacturers such as Cadbury in Victorian society). It could also be taught from a geographic perspective (where and how cocoa beans are grown and how they are transported), a scientific perspective (investigating the melting point of chocolate), a literacy perspective (reading *Charlie and the Chocolate Factory*) or a nutritional perspective (looking at the nutritional content of chocolate).

This approach is known as the 'creative curriculum' and has already been adopted in some primary schools. The creative curriculum approach has been broadly welcomed by teachers and educationists because it offers teachers greater freedom to tailor the curriculum to the interests of the children. Teachers will still be expected to make sure children learn specific skills and knowledge within the context of the creative curriculum.

After the publication of the *Independent Review of the Primary Curriculum* by Sir Jim Rose in 2009, the last government decided to formalise the creative curriculum approach and to introduce a new curriculum from September 2011. The change of government means that plans for a new curriculum are unlikely to go ahead. The new government may, however, make other changes to the curriculum.

Wales, Scotland and Northern Ireland

The curricula for Wales, Scotland and Northern Ireland are set by their own regional governments, and so differ from the one for England. Here is a brief description for each country. You can find links directing you to further information in the help list.

Wales

As in England, the primary National Curriculum is divided into Early Years, KS1 (Years 1 and 2) and KS2 (Years 3-6), and covers the same 11 subject areas (including RE) as the English National Curriculum. There is also the addition of Welsh, either as a first or second language. Children are assessed using the same system of levels used in England. However, children in Wales do not take SATs, and teachers carry out assessments at seven and 11 years old. See the help list for sources of further information on the Welsh National Curriculum.

Scotland

Scotland is in the process of implementing a new curriculum called Curriculum for Excellence. It aims to be less prescriptive than the old curriculum, giving teachers more freedom to choose which subjects to teach and how to teach them. There will be more cross-curricular teaching, as in the new curriculum in England. The curriculum is divided into eight areas:

- Expressive arts.
- Health and wellbeing.
- Languages.
- Mathematics.
- Religious and moral education.
- Sciences.
- Social studies.
- Technologies.

Pupils in Scotland do not sit SATs. Teachers administer national tests to pupils when they think they have reached a certain level. The teachers mark these tests and the results are not published. See the help list for sources of further information on the Scottish National Curriculum.

Northern Ireland

The National Curriculum in Northern Ireland is similar to that in England and Wales. It uses the same terminology of Early Years, KS1 and KS2.

There are no SATs, but teachers carry out yearly pupil assessments. They then produce an annual individual pupil profile for parents based on these assessments. See the help list for sources of further information on the Northern Irish National Curriculum.

Summing Up

- The National Curriculum sets out the subjects that should be taught, and how they should be taught, in primary schools throughout England.

- There are three core subjects (maths, literacy and science) and seven foundation subjects.

- Children are assessed on their achievements in the core subjects at seven and 11 years old. At age 11, this is through sitting formal tests known as SATs.

- Schools monitor children's progress closely, and you can expect to receive an annual school report and have twice-yearly consultation meetings with the school.

- Scotland, Wales and Northern Ireland all set their own curricula, though in Wales and Northern Ireland these are similar to the one used in England.

Chapter Five

The Foundation Stage (3-5 years old)

Introduction

The foundation stage covers children aged 3-5, when children are in nursery or reception class. Nursery isn't compulsory, but if your child is in either a private pre-school or a nursery class attached to a primary school, they will be following the curriculum for the foundation stage.

The foundation stage is part of the EYFS, which covers children aged 0-5. EYFS is a framework for childminders, nurseries and schools that outlines developmental goals for children. The government's aim in creating the EYFS was to make sure that children from deprived backgrounds had the opportunity to learn the same skills as children from better-off backgrounds. However, it has been controversial because it specifies learning goals for very young children, who may naturally develop at different rates.

In this chapter, we look at how you can prepare your child for the foundation stage and what your child will be doing.

The foundation stage is broken into six areas of learning and development, each of which includes a set of early learning goals. This chapter will look at what children will be learning in each area and how they will be assessed.

Six areas of learning and development

The six areas are:

- Personal, social and emotional development.
- Communication, language and literacy.
- Problem solving, reasoning and numeracy.
- Knowledge and understanding of the world.
- Physical development.
- Creative development.

Although this sounds a daunting curriculum for three- and four-year-olds, in reality the emphasis will be on learning through play. Don't expect your child to be doing masses of work!

Personal, social and emotional development

This is all about getting children to acquire social skills. It includes things like playing with other children, taking turns fairly, respecting the needs of others, developing a desire to learn, sitting quietly when the teacher is talking, going to the toilet by themselves and understanding why it's not acceptable to hit another child. These are set out as a series of 15 early learning goals that include being able to:

- Have a developing awareness of their own needs, views and feelings, and be sensitive to the needs, views and feelings of others.
- Dress and undress independently and manage their own personal hygiene.
- Respond to significant experiences, showing a range of feelings when appropriate.
- Work as part of a group or class, taking turns and sharing fairly, understanding that there needs to be agreed values and codes of behaviour for groups of people, including adults and children, to work together harmoniously.

You may think some of these are a tall order! Children develop at different rates, and not all five-year-olds are confident about getting dressed and undressed or are good at sitting still, let alone 'responding to significant experiences'. You can help your child by encouraging them to get dressed on their own at home and introducing times when they are expected to sit quietly on their own to get on with an activity. Providing your child with opportunities to mix with other children (such as going to playgroups) can also help. But don't worry too much – your child will learn these skills eventually. Some children surprise their parents by being much better behaved at school than they are at home.

Kerry's eldest son struggled in his first few weeks in reception class: '"He doesn't understand about rules or sharing" the class teacher told me with some concern, clearly wondering if I was a hippy mum who let him run riot at home. A few days later, the breakthrough came. "Mummy, there are rules at school now, you can't run inside or shout! The teacher told me! She told me specially!" Far from feeling imprisoned by school boundaries, my excitable son welcomed them. They made sense of a new experience, made him feel secure.'

Communication, language and literacy

'Literacy' at this age doesn't mean learning to read and write. The early years curriculum is all about encouraging children to talk, to listen, to learn new words, to enjoy nursery rhymes and stories and to form their letters. These activities are an important foundation for learning to read and write, but they're also important in themselves – the emphasis on talking and listening continues to be part of the National Curriculum throughout primary school and secondary school.

In nursery or reception, children might spend time using tweezers to pick up little beads, which is a good way of developing fine motor control necessary for writing. They might also practise writing big letters in the air with their hands, so they can learn the shape they make.

Some of the things that children should be able to do by the end of foundation stage (when they are five years old) include:

'With F, I "taught" him letter sounds in various ways – potato prints, foam bath letters and so on. We also used to read our way round our neighbourhood, "Private drive – no parking at any time" was the first sentence he read when he was two or so.'

Rachel, mum of two.

- Enjoy listening to and using spoken and written language, and readily turn to it in their play and learning.

- Use their phonic knowledge to write simple regular words and make phonetically plausible attempts at more complex words.

- Retell narratives in the correct sequence, drawing on language patterns of stories.

- Write their own names and other things such as labels and captions, and begin to form simple sentences, sometimes using punctuation.

- Use talk to organise, sequence and clarify thinking, ideas, feelings and events.

'The most important thing is reading with and to your child from birth, talking and singing rhymes. The children who can rhyme seem to be able to read.'

Mrs W, KS1 teacher.

The National Curriculum now requires children to learn to read using a system called 'phonics'. We'll say more about this in the next chapter, but in essence it means learning to associate letters with the sound they make, so children can work out, for example, that 'c-a-t' spells cat. Research has shown the use of phonics to be more effective than other methods of teaching children to read (such as teaching them to recognise whole words), though it has its detractors.

There are lots of ways you can help your child's literacy and communication skills:

- Read stories to your child from an early age – even babies can enjoy stories. An interest in narrative will spark an interest in reading.

- Let your child handle books: pop-up books or books with textures are fun for small children.

- Talk to your child. It sounds obvious, yet it's easy to become so caught up in our lives that we forget to have proper conversations with our children.

- Encourage your child to draw pictures, to do jigsaws and play with building blocks and Lego – these all help to develop the motor skills necessary for writing.

- Sing songs and recite nursery rhymes to your child, encouraging them to join in – this is a good way of helping children not only to remember words but to enjoy using them.

Problem solving, reasoning and numeracy

This learning and development area is about developing simple number skills and basic mathematical concepts, such as shape and distance. The 12 early learning goals include the ability to:

- Count reliably up to 10 everyday objects.

- Use language such as 'more' or 'less' to compare two numbers.

- Find one more or one less than a number from one to 10.

- Begin to relate addition to combining two groups of objects and subtraction to 'taking away'.

- Use language such as 'greater', 'smaller', 'heavier' or 'lighter' to compare quantities.

You can help your child by:

- Singing and reciting number rhymes together (e.g. 'one, two, three, four, five, once I caught a fish alive').

- Playing games that involve counting or using dice, such as Snakes and Ladders.

- Counting objects with your child in day-to-day situations, such as the number of forks on a table, or the number of biscuits on a plate.

'With F, I did all the obvious things – counting out potatoes in Sainsbury's, and counting how many steps we went down.'

Rachel, mum of two.

Knowledge and understanding of the world

This covers the very beginnings of understanding about how to carry about research: children learn how to develop the very basic skills needed to explore and make sense of the world, whether it's the physical environment, the past or other cultures. It's all about harnessing children's natural curiosity and showing them how to use that curiosity to find out more. Some of the early learning goals include the ability to:

- Investigate objects and materials by using all of their senses as appropriate. Find out about and identify some features of living things, objects and events they observe.

- Look closely at similarities, differences, patterns and change. Ask questions about why things happen and how things work.

- Find out about and identify the uses of everyday technology and use ICT and programmable toys to support their learning.

- Find out about past and present events in their own lives and in those of their families and other people they know.

This will also include traditional activities such as playing with clay or with sand and water, growing plants in window boxes, and dissolving and mixing substances.

You can help your child by:

- Engaging with your child's own curiosity. Small children love to ask questions: 'How do spiders make webs?' 'Was Grandma alive at the time of the dinosaurs?' 'Where do stones come from?' Try answering questions in a way that your child will understand – and if you don't know the answer, try to look it up together, using the Internet or the library.

- Carrying out some simple scientific experiments. You can work out what floats and what sinks, for example, by filling up a basin of water and throwing in different objects. Messy, but fun.

- Growing cress at home – easy to do with a packet of seeds and some wet cotton wool.

- Playing some simple computer games with your child, such as those on the BBC's Cbeebies website (see help list).

Physical development

Physical development covers both physical abilities (such as control and co-ordination of movement) and physical awareness, such as knowing the importance of eating healthy food. Children will start to perform simple PE tasks, such as balancing on play equipment, and learn to handle tools like scissors. Here are some of the early learning goals:

- Move with confidence, imagination and in safety.

- Show awareness of space, of themselves and of others.

- Recognise the importance of keeping healthy and those things which contribute to this.

- Recognise the changes that happen to their bodies when they are active.

- Use a range of small and large equipment.

You can help your child by making opportunities for physical play out of school, whether it's walks to the park, trampolining or learning to ride a bicycle. Most children enjoy physical play, so won't need too much encouragement.

Creative development

Creative development covers art, music, story telling, rhymes, singing, dance and drama. It's about fostering children's innate creativity so they feel confident about using their imagination, whether it's to make up a dance, to invent a story or to act out role plays. Early learning goals include:

- Respond in a variety of ways to what they see, hear, smell, touch and feel.

- Express and communicate their ideas, thoughts and feelings by using a widening range of materials, suitable tools, imagination and role-play, movement, designing and making, and a variety of songs and musical instruments.

- Explore colour, texture, shape, form and space in two or three dimensions.

- Recognise and explore how sounds can be changed, sing simple songs from memory, recognise repeated sounds and sound patterns, and match movements to music.

- Use their imagination in art and design, music, dance, role-play and stories.

You can help your child by:

- Reading stories at home and asking your child to guess the ending or make up their own ending.

- Singing songs together and maybe accompanying them with simple musical instruments like tambourines and drums

- Providing a dressing-up box so your child can role-play stories.

- Providing plenty of paper, pencils and crayons and encouraging your child to draw.

'We were invited to a parents' event to view classroom work. I was astonished to see my son's drawing: careful and neat. At home, any suggestion that he draw was met with eye-rolling, groans and a reluctant unidentifiable scribble.'

Kerry, mum of three.

Assessment

Your child's teachers will monitor your child's progress throughout the foundation stage. At the end of the stage, when your child has completed the reception year, the teachers will complete an EYFS profile that provides an assessment of how your child has performed against the early learning goals. As a parent, you will be given a summary of the profile information, though you have the right to see the full profile if you want it.

The teachers make their assessments with reference to a document called the Assessment Scales Reference Sheet. Each of the six learning areas is assessed on a 9-point scale. Some are divided into subsections, making a total of 13 areas in which your child is assessed.

'I am amazed that teachers can actually teach with all the assessment that has to be done. When my son was in the foundation stage, he was marked down in some areas because he didn't play with certain types of toys – he just played with his favourite.'

Claire, mum of two.

Six learning areas	Subsections
Personal, social and emotional development	Dispositions and attitudes
	Social development
	Emotional development
Communication, language and literacy	Language for communication and thinking
	Linking letters and sounds
	Reading
	Writing
Problem solving, reasoning and numeracy	Numbers as labels and for counting
	Calculating
	Shape, space and measures
Knowledge and understanding of the world	
Physical development	
Creative development	

(© QCDA, Early Years Foundation Stage Profile – Assessment Scales Reference Sheet.)

In each of these 13 areas, there are nine levels. If your child only achieves levels 1-3, then they are still working towards the early learning goals. If they achieve levels 4-8, then they have reached the targets set for that age group. If they achieve level 9, then they are working beyond the level of the early learning targets – in other words, they are performing above average for that age group.

This is all rather complicated, so the table below should make it a little clearer. The table shows the assessment scales for 'language for communication and thinking', which is one of the four subsections of the 'communication, language and literacy' learning area (see previous table).

Scale point	Language for communication and thinking
1	Listens and responds.
2	Initiates communication with others, displaying greater confidence in more informal contexts.
3	Talks activities through, reflecting on and modifying actions.
4	Listens with enjoyment to stories, songs, rhymes and poems, sustains attentive listening and responds with relevant comments, questions or actions.
5	Uses language to imagine and recreate roles and experiences.
6	Interacts with others in a variety of contexts, negotiating plans and activities and taking turns in conversation.
7	Uses talk to organise, sequence and clarify thinking, ideas, feelings and events, exploring the meanings and sounds of new words.
8	Speaks clearly with confidence and control, showing awareness of the listener.
9	Talks and listens confidently and with control, consistently showing awareness of the listener by including relevant detail. Uses language to work out and clarify ideas, showing control of a range of appropriate vocabulary.

(© QCDA, Early Years Foundation Stage Profile – Assessment Scales Reference Sheet.)

Summing Up

- The foundation stage covers the years your child is in nursery class and reception class.

- The foundation stage covers six broad areas of learning, each of which has a set of early learning goals.

- At this stage, your child will mainly be learning through play.

- At the end of the reception year, the teacher will complete an EYFS profile for your child that gives an assessment of how they are progressing against the early learning goals.

Chapter Six

Key Stage 1 (5-7 years old)

Introduction

In the foundation stage, children learn mostly through play. When they enter Year 1, they embark on a more formal course of learning. It can be a difficult adjustment for some children, so your child may need extra help from you.

In KS1, which spans Years 1 and 2, children are taught 11 subjects:

- Literacy.
- Maths.
- Science.
- Design and technology.
- ICT.
- History.
- Geography.
- Art and design.
- Music.
- PE.
- RE.

Although RE is a statutory subject, it has a non-statutory programme of study – which means that schools don't have to follow a standard curriculum.

PSHE is a non-statutory subject, which means that schools are not obliged to teach it, though some do. PSHE covers things like emotional development (how to express your feelings), social skills (the importance of respecting the feelings of others), citizenship (understanding and following agreed rules for behaviour in and out of class) and staying healthy (eating healthy foods and the importance of personal hygiene).

In this chapter, we'll focus mainly on literacy, maths and science, with a brief outline of what you can expect in the other subjects.

'My son had a big shock when he started Year 1 as there was less playing, but he is enjoying the subjects – writing, spelling, science, maths and PE.'

Claire, mum of two.

Programmes of study

Each subject has a programme of study, consisting of two elements:

- Knowledge, skills and understanding. This is about what children learn – e.g. understanding how narrative works.
- Breadth of study. This is about how children learn – e.g. through reading fairy stories or writing their own stories.

Let's take literacy as an example, which has a speaking and listening component. The knowledge, skills and understanding elements for speaking, as described in the QCDA programme of study, say that includes being able to 'choose words with precision' and 'focus on the main point'. The breadth of study – which is about how they learn the skills – includes 'telling stories, real and imagined' and 'reading aloud and reciting'.

The programmes of study for each subject are lengthy and detailed, so this chapter will just give an overview of what your child can expect to learn in each subject. There is a help list at the end of this book that will enable you to find out more.

Literacy

Your child can expect to spend at least an hour a day engaged in literacy activities. It used to be a requirement that schools spent a fixed hour each day teaching literacy, but now schools are encouraged to integrate literacy with other curriculum subjects. For example, in a history session about Victorian toys, your child might be asked to take part in a role play about the games played by a Victorian child, or write a story involving a Victorian child opening his Christmas presents.

Literacy will be taught in blocks lasting several weeks. In Year 1, for example, children will spend 16-17 weeks on narrative, 12 weeks on non-fiction and six weeks on poetry. Each block is further broken down into units, so in the third block, poetry, children will spend two weeks on using the senses, two weeks on pattern and rhyme and two weeks on poems with a theme.

In each block, children will be working on three skills:

- Speaking and listening.
- Reading.
- Writing.

Speaking and listening

Speaking and listening is all about learning the basics of social interaction: speaking clearly, taking part in group discussions, listening to what others say, asking questions and taking different views into account. There's also a drama element where children learn to role-play characters – perhaps acting out the story of *Goldilocks and the Three Bears*, or making up a situation such as a child nagging her mum to buy her a toy in the shop.

Reading

Some children will enter KS1 already able to read. For those who can't, the process of learning to read starts in earnest. Each week there will be some sessions of whole class teaching, some sessions where the teacher

'Speaking and listening is all about learning the basics of social interaction: speaking clearly, taking part in group discussions, listening to what others say, asking questions and taking different views into account.'

or teaching assistant listens to each child read out loud, and some 'guided reading' sessions, usually lasting about 20 minutes, where a group of children of similar reading ability sit at the same table reading from the same book.

In a guided reading session, the teacher begins by talking about the book to the children, discussing the pictures and the story and picking out words that might be tricky. The children then read individually and the teacher asks them questions to assess their comprehension and help them with words they find difficult. While a teacher sits with a group doing guided reading, the other children in the class are usually engaged in other literacy activities.

Most KS1 teachers will also have a storytime session at the end of the day, in which the teacher reads a story to the children.

The literacy programme of study says that children should be taught to read using different methods:

Phonics

This is the main method used in teaching reading. It consists of matching letters and combinations of letters to particular sounds, so children learn that 'c-a-t' spells 'cat' and that 'c-h-a-t' spells 'chat.' Phonics is generally regarded as the most successful way of teaching children to read, although some children benefit from a mix of methods.

Two approaches can be used to teaching phonics: synthetic phonics and analytic phonics. Recent research suggests that synthetic phonics is the more effective approach.

- Synthetic phonics: children learn 44 phonemes (pronounced foh-neem). A phoneme is a unit of sound, such as 'S' or 'OW' or 'SH'. Each phoneme has a related grapheme (pronounced graf-eem) which is a written representation of the sound. A single phoneme may have more than one grapheme. For example, you can represent the sound 'ee' as 'ee' or 'ei' or 'ea', and the words 'read,' 'reid' and 'reed' all sound the same. Children are taught to recognise the grapheme and then associate it with the sound it makes.

- Analytic phonics: now less popular than synthetic phonics, it emphasises individual letters rather than sounds, and encourages children to use rhyme to help them work out certain words. For example, if you can read 'sight,' the idea is that you can then recognise 'might' or 'light'.

Although phonics is the main method used, teachers are still expected to help children through other methods.

Word recognition

This involves learning to recognise high-frequency words on sight. So rather than sound the word out, children learn to recognise common words like 'the', 'and', 'boy', 'girl' and so on. Word recognition is useful for words where the spelling doesn't match the sound, such as 'light'.

Grammatical awareness

Developing a rudimentary understanding of grammar helps children recognise the next word in a sentence. Take 'The boys played with their trains.' The child can anticipate the word 'their' because it follows on logically from 'the boys'.

Contextual understanding

This is about teaching children to use their awareness of context to read words. The context could be what happened in the previous chapter, or what's shown in the picture. So if the picture shows a toy train, this can help the child guess at the word 'train' in the example above.

KS1 literacy isn't just about teaching children to read – it's about helping them to enjoy reading and to use it to gather information. So your child's teacher will be encouraging pupils to talk about the books they've read, explaining why they have or haven't enjoyed them, to act out stories, to recite poems and to respond imaginatively to what they've read by, for example, writing a poem with a similar structure or writing a story about one of the characters from a book. The breadth of study – the curriculum content, in other words – will include things like fairy stories, stories by well-known children's authors, poems and folk tales.

In KS1, your child will regularly bring home reading books, usually based on a reading scheme such as the Oxford Reading Tree. The teacher will encourage you to listen to your child reading once a day and to fill in a reading record book. The best time to listen to your child read is when they are feeling alert, so doing it soon after school finishes (or even first thing in the morning, if you have time) is a better idea than doing it last thing before bedtime.

Schemes like the Oxford Reading Tree operate on a colour coding scheme, where stage one is grey, stage two is green, stage three is blue and so on. It's very easy to get obsessed by the stage your child is at.

Mrs W, a KS1 teacher, says: 'With reading books, parents do get very hung up on the colour band, and they see their progress in terms of what reading book they're bringing home. We say to parents, "If they've read the book and finished it, go to the library, read as many different books as you can – you don't just have to read the reading scheme book."'

'Surreptitious reading can take place through reading labels on food, word searches and word puzzles.'

Hannah, mum of two.

What if my child is slow to read?

There are different reasons why a child may be slow to read. Summer-born children (some of whom may have only spent two terms in reception class) will usually take longer than autumn-born children, and boys as a rule pick up reading less quickly than girls.

One of the biggest success factors in learning anything is motivation. Children are much more likely to learn to read if they want to read. So introduce them to the pleasure of stories by reading to them each night, if you can. If you read a lot yourself, that encourages them to see reading as both normal and enjoyable. Carry on singing songs and nursery rhymes. If your child is enthusiastic, then you can have fun when you're out and about pointing at signs and asking your child to work out what they say. But don't do it if it just induces stress and anxiety.

There are a couple of other possibilities:

- Your child may have a learning disability such as dyslexia. If you suspect this to be the case, you need to talk to your child's teacher about it and try to get an independent assessment. See *Dyslexia and Other Learning Difficulties – A Parent's Guide* (Need2Know).

- Your child may simply not be ready to read yet. In the UK, we start teaching children to read at a very young age in comparison with other countries. While some children learn quite quickly, other children, who may otherwise be very bright, don't 'click' with reading until they're seven or eight years old and then pick it up very quickly.

Writing

Learning to write is partly about learning to form the letters, first writing them separately and then joining them up. But it's also about learning to punctuate, learning to spell correctly and learning to communicate your ideas and thoughts coherently. It's a complicated set of skills.

Your child will be taught five core skills:

- Composition.
- Planning and drafting.
- Punctuation.
- Spelling.
- Handwriting and presentation.

The breadth of study – the way your child will learn the above skills – includes communicating to others, creating imaginary worlds, explaining information and exploring experiences and organisation.

Many children at this age have difficulty with handwriting. As with reading, boys tend to be slower than girls, and summer-born children will as a rule be behind autumn-born children. Learning to write is partly a matter of physical strength and co-ordination, so don't worry too much if your child struggles. Playing with toys such as Lego and Meccano can help children acquire the fine motor skills necessary to write with confidence.

Some schools introduce regular spelling tests at KS1, while some choose not to. While spelling is important, try not to worry if your child is a poor speller. Anxiety about spelling can inhibit your child's writing and make them avoid spelling words they have difficulty with. At this age, encouraging fluency is more important than making sure the spelling is right.

Meanwhile, you can help with spelling by encouraging reading, whether it's books, comics or signs in shops. Reading and spelling skills often (but not always) go hand in hand.

Mathematics

As with literacy, maths is taught in blocks, each lasting a fixed number of weeks. In Year 1, there are five blocks, each of which is divided into three units. Teachers have to teach the five blocks in order throughout the school year.

Although it's divided into numerous blocks and units, the maths curriculum for KS1 is focused on two principal areas:

- Number.
- Shape, space and measures.

Number

Number is further subdivided into:

- Using and applying number.
- Numbers and the number system.
- Calculations.
- Solving numerical problems.
- Processing, representing and interpreting data.

In practice, this means that children learn to count beyond 10, starting with the numbers 11 to 20, and then gradually going up to 100 and beyond. They learn to add and subtract numbers and to recognise the plus and minus symbols.

They also learn the difference between odd and even numbers, to recognise the patterns of the multiples 2, 5 and 10 (e.g. being able to count up in 10s) and to recognise the relationship between halving and doubling.

Children will learn to carry out simple sums such as:

$$5 + 3 = ?$$

$$? + 3 = 8$$

They'll also learn simple mathematical concepts so that they understand, for example, that multiplication is repeated addition and that 5 x 3 could also be represented as 5+5+5.

They'll also learn strategies for helping them solve mathematical problems, such as adding a zero when they want to multiply a number by 10.

Children will learn the basics of representing data in different formats, such as tables and graphs, and to answer questions about them.

Shape, space and measures

This has four components:

- Using and applying shape, space and measures.

- Understanding patterns and properties of shape.

- Understanding properties of position and movement.

- Understanding measures.

This is all about learning to understand shape and measurement, so children will learn to recognise and to create basic 2D and 3D shapes, such as squares and triangles, cubes and pyramids.

'Children will learn the basics of representing data in different formats, such as tables and graphs, and to answer questions about them.'

They'll also learn the skills of measuring in the metric system (centimetres, kilograms and litres) and to use measuring tools such as a ruler, a measuring jug or a set of scales. They'll learn to estimate the size of objects and to compare the measurements of different objects.

Children will begin to learn how to describe the position of an object, to recognise movement in a straight line or in rotation (so that they can say, for example, which way a toy will face if you half-turn it) and to recognise right angles.

'The science curriculum isn't just about learning important scientific facts. It's about learning how to be a scientist: how to carry out experiments, how to make observations and how to collect evidence.'

Breadth of study

The breadth of study for maths says that children should learn maths through practical activities, such as counting money, playing shop or carrying out measurements. They might learn about measurement through measuring every child in the class, or perhaps measuring their hands or feet. The results can be displayed in a graph.

One way you can help your child is by playing shop with them. Small children often find it hard to grasp the idea that coins are of a different value – e.g. that a 5p coin is worth more than a 1p coin. To give your child extra encouragement, set up a pretend toyshop at home using toys you already have in the house, attach labels to them for different amounts and take turns being the shopkeeper.

You can also use rulers to measure different objects around the house – finding out which teddy is tallest, for example.

Science

The science curriculum in KS1 isn't just about learning important scientific facts. It's about learning how to be a scientist: how to carry out experiments, how to make observations and how to collect evidence. The topics covered map broadly onto the three disciplines of biology, chemistry and physics.

Here are the four main areas of KS1 science:

- Scientific enquiry.

- Life processes and living things.
- Materials and their properties.
- Physical processes.

Scientific enquiry

Children learn to ask questions and think about how to find the answers to them. They learn to obtain, present and evaluate evidence (by recording measurements, for example, and presenting them as a graph) and to identify simple patterns.

Life processes and living things

Children learn basic biological principles, grouped under five main categories: life processes; humans and other animals; green plants; variation and classification; and living things in their environment. So they'll learn the difference between living and non-living things, the need for humans and animals to eat and drink to stay alive, the need for plants to have light and water to grow, and that seeds grow into plants.

There is also an element of learning about responsibility in this part of the curriculum. Children will learn about the importance of healthy eating and exercise, about how to treat animals with care and sensitivity, how to recognise similarities and differences between themselves and others, and how to treat other people with sensitivity.

Materials and their properties

Children learn both to group materials (e.g. sort materials into groups based on their physical properties) and to change materials (e.g. by twisting or stretching them, or understanding how water turns into ice when cooled or chocolate melts when heated).

Physical processes

Children learn some of the basics of physics:

- Electricity – this includes knowing which appliances use electricity and how to make a simple electrical circuit.

- Forces and motion – this includes being able to describe the movement of familiar things (e.g. cars going faster, slowing down, changing direction).

- Light and sound – this includes being able to identify different light sources, understanding that darkness is the absence of light and being aware that sounds travel away from sources, getting fainter as they do so.

Breadth of study

Children are taught about science through familiar objects and settings – a car, for example, or a light bulb or a kettle. They learn about the role science has played in developing things we use today, and develop the skill of using different sources of information and data. They are expected to learn to use simple scientific language to communicate ideas and to describe 'living things, materials, phenomena and processes'. They will also learn the basics of health and safety, such as how to reduce risk to themselves and others.

Other subjects

The other subjects your child will study in KS1 are:

- Design and technology.
- ICT.
- History.
- Geography.
- Art and design.
- Music.
- PE.

Teachers have more freedom about how much time they spend on these subjects, and when they teach them, than they do for the three core subjects. For example, teachers might decide to teach history for two terms and geography for a third term, or they might decide to teach both history and geography.

A lot of emphasis is put in the curriculum on children as active rather than passive learners – finding information out for themselves and developing skills of evaluation and analysis rather than simply learning facts about different subjects. These skills are taught through topics. For example, in history typical topics for KS1 children include:

- Famous events, like the Great Fire of London.

- Famous people, such as Florence Nightingale.

- Beyond living memory – what life was like in the past (e.g. the kinds of houses people lived in 100 years ago).

- In living memory – what life was like in the recent past (e.g. what a day at the seaside might have been like for our parents and grandparents).

In geography, children will learn to:

- Ask geographical questions, such as 'What is it like to live in this place?'

- Use geographical vocabulary, such as north and south.

- Use globes and maps.

Similarly, in art and design children have the opportunity to create works of art for themselves, using different materials – so they'll learn to draw and paint, create objects from dough, make prints and work with fabrics.

Links to more information about the contents of the KS1 curriculum can be found in the help list.

Summing Up

- In KS1, children learn 11 subjects.

- Each subject has a programme of study which outlines what children will learn in each subject.

- Teachers will spend at least an hour a day on literacy and maths.

- Reading is taught by a range of methods, but principally using phonics.

- The curriculum encourages children to become active learners, finding things out for themselves.

Chapter Seven

Key Stage 1 SATs

Taking SATs

Towards the end of Year 2, when your child is seven or nearly seven, they will sit KS1 SATs in maths and literacy (but only the reading and writing components). These are not external examinations. The teacher will give the pupils a series of tests to assess their progress, and the tests will last for less than three hours in total. Ideally, these should be informal – pupils may not even know they are taking SATs.

To make sure that teachers are marking pupils fairly and accurately, schools send marked papers to the LA for external moderation.

What happens in the tests?

Reading

Your child will be asked to read a passage to a teacher or teaching assistant from a list of approved books. After reading, the teacher will ask some questions to see how much your child has understood.

There will also be a written comprehension test – your child will be given a booklet containing a story and some non-fiction writing, which they will be expected to read and then answer questions about in writing. More able children will be tested with a harder comprehension booklet.

Writing

Children will be given another booklet in which they write down words when the teacher calls them out – a standard spelling test.

Children will also be asked to do two pieces of writing. The writing will be marked on how well your child can:

- Describe and explain things.
- Plan a piece of work.
- Spell.
- Use punctuation.
- Use joined-up writing.

Maths

Children will be given a booklet of maths questions based on the work they have done in maths lessons, covering topics such as addition, multiplication, measuring and fractions. Typical questions might be:

- $5 + 9 + 7 + 4 = ?$
- Write the missing numbers in this sequence:

  2   4   6   ?   10   12   ?   16
- Stacey wants to buy a bar of chocolate. It costs 50p. She has 30p. How much more money does she need?
- Here are some numbers. Put them in order from smallest to largest:

  25   38   73   19   47
- Tommy has 15 marbles. He puts them into groups of five. How many groups of five can he make altogether?

Need2Know

More able children – those working at level 3 – will be given a second booklet, with more difficult questions. Typical questions might be:

- Here are some signs:

  +   –   ×   =

  Which sign do you need to make the sum correct?

  10   3   30

- $159 + 32 = ?$

- Nikita spends three hours each week doing her two out-of-school activities: Brownies and ballet. She spends 75 minutes doing ballet. How many minutes does she spend doing Brownies?

- Harry had £10. He spent £3.45. How much money did he have left?

Teacher assessment

As well as taking written tests, pupils are assessed by teachers on the work they've been doing in class throughout the year. Five areas are assessed:

- Reading.
- Writing.
- Speaking and listening.
- Maths.
- Science.

SATs scores

In most schools, parents will receive a report at the end of Year 2 giving their child's scores in each of the subjects covered in the SATs. The scores reflect your child's progress throughout the year, not just how they did in the tests themselves.

There are three levels, going from 1 (the lowest level) to 3 (the highest level). Some pupils with special needs will not reach level 1, and a separate scale, known as the P scale, is used for these children.

Most children are expected to achieve level 2 in each subject. A smaller number of more able children will achieve level 3, while lower achieving children may only achieve level 1. Even an academically brilliant child will not achieve a level 4 unless the school allows them to take a level 4 paper (usually only taken by Year 6 children).

Level 2 is further subdivided into 'a', 'b' and 'c', where 'a' is the highest and 'c' is the lowest.

Here is what the scores mean:

Scores	Meaning
1	Achieving below the target for age seven.
2c	Working towards the expected standard for age seven.
2b	At the expected standard for age seven.
2a	Working easily within the expected standard, and nearly at the next stage.
3	Working above the expected standard for age seven.

To give an idea of the difference between the levels, the QCDA have summaries on their website (http://curriculum.qcda.gov.uk) for each subject. The summaries help you understand exactly what it is your child can do, and what they need to aim for in the future. Click on to 'primary curriculum', then 'subjects' to view a list of KS1 and KS2 subjects. Each one will have an 'attainment target' in the menu that appears when a subject is clicked on.

How much do SATs tell me?

It's worth bearing in mind two things:

- Children develop at different rates, so a SATs score is a guide rather than a definitive measure of your child's academic ability.

- Date of birth can make a big difference. An August-born child will be nearly a year younger than some children in the same class. This is why it can help to ask your school for your child's age-standardised score, though not all schools provide them. Age-standardised scores are explained in more detail below.

Measuring your child's progress

Many schools continue giving children tests designed by the QCDA outside the two SATs years (Years 2 and 6) to assess how they are progressing. On average, a child is expected to progress two sub-levels each year, so a child who achieves level 2a in Year 2 would be expected to achieve level 3b by the end of Year 3, and 4a by the end of Year 6. Of course, not all children progress at an average rate, so this is just a guideline.

Age-standardised scores

Some, but not all, schools like to calculate a child's age-standardised score as well as the SATs score. An age-standardised score takes into account your child's age and recognises the fact that children born later in the academic year on average do less well than children born at the beginning of the academic year. Teachers use a special table to convert the SATs score into an age-standardised score.

An average age-standardised score is 100, and two thirds of pupils will fall in the range between 85 and 115.

Not all schools will share the age-standardised scores with parents. You can ask to see the scores, but the school is not obliged to give them to you.

How to prepare your child for SATs

SATs are not exams that your child can pass or fail. The aim of SATs is to assess the school's ability to teach its pupils, rather than to grade each child. So while it's a good idea to help your child do well at school, and encourage and help them with schoolwork, coaching specifically for the tests is not a good idea, and is more likely to make your child feel stressed than help them

'Parents often worry that their child's not making progress because of the SATs and they believe they must be achieving 2b at the end of Year 2, but children don't progress in a steady way – they can plateau out and then shoot up. It's very hard for parents.'

Mrs W, KS1 teacher.

to do well. Although you can buy practice papers online, they don't have a particular value – unless your child is the type who enjoys doing tests and can treat them as fun.

You can help your child by listening to them read out loud or by asking questions about what has been read. You can also help them practise writing – perhaps by asking them to write a story or help you with your shopping list. Similarly, maths activities can be integrated into everyday life, as suggested in earlier chapters.

Summing Up

- Your child will sit SATs papers in literacy and maths near the end of Year 2, when they are seven or nearly seven.

- The papers are marked by teachers, not external examiners.

- SATs scores are represented as levels (1, 2a, 2b, 2c and 3).

- The expected standard for this age is 2b.

- Children vary a good deal in their rates of development, so a low score isn't necessarily a cause for concern.

Chapter Eight

Key Stage 2
(7–11 years old)

Introduction

In KS2, which spans Years 3 to 6, children are taught the same 11 subjects as in KS1, plus one other – modern foreign languages, which becomes compulsory in September 2010. Schools can choose which modern foreign language to teach, though in most cases it will probably be French.

As in KS1, PSHE is currently non-statutory. RE remains a statutory subject with a non-statutory curriculum.

Also, as in KS1, each subject has a programme of study consisting of two elements: knowledge, skills and understanding (what children learn), and breadth of study (how children learn).

In KS2, your child may also receive sex education lessons. Currently, every primary school must provide a written statement of their policy on sex education and make it available to parents and pupils. Parents can choose to withdraw their children from all or part of sex education lessons.

The last government had plans to make sex and relationships education a statutory part of the National Curriculum from 2011. These plans now seem unlikely to go ahead.

In this chapter, we'll focus mainly on literacy, maths and science, with a brief outline of what you can expect in the other subjects. Because the curriculum goes into a lot of detail, we won't have the space to include everything, but useful sources of information are listed in the help list.

Literacy

As at KS1, children will spend an hour a day on literacy. There are three components:

- Speaking and listening.
- Reading.
- Writing.

Teachers are expected to make sure that work in these three areas is integrated.

Literacy is typically taught in three- or four-week blocks. In one block, children will learn about a particular type of communication or narrative, such as myth, poetry, drama, persuasive writing or instructions. In each block, they will do some speaking and listening, some reading and some writing (not necessarily in that order, though the blocks always finish with a piece of extended writing).

For example, if they are studying instructions, they might begin by listening to instructions; then acting instructions out using role-play; then reading instructions, such as recipes, manuals or help text. Following this they might discuss the particular features that characterise instructions (numbered lists, for example); then, finally, they will write their own instructions.

Speaking and listening

Speaking and listening skills become more advanced, as you would expect, in KS2.

Children will learn how to adapt their speaking styles, e.g. by choosing material that is appropriate for their audience, or by altering the pace of their speech or introducing humour to hold an audience's attention.

They also learn how to take part in a group discussion – about the importance of taking turns, how to listen to other people's point of view – and take up roles such as chair or minute-taker. Listening is a related skill – children learn to identify the key points in a discussion, ask relevant questions and summarise what others have said.

'Those children who find writing very difficult, but who have a lot to offer, can offer it through drama and speaking and listening. You find out that they know things that you wouldn't normally have picked up through their writing.'

Mr S, KS2 teacher.

Need2Know

Drama becomes an important component of speaking and listening at KS2, with children learning to script short plays and act out roles.

At this stage, children also learn the difference between standard English and dialect forms of English, and when it is appropriate to vary their language – understanding, for example, that written English needs to be more formal than spoken English.

Expect your child to start taking part in a range of activities that involve speaking and listening: making presentations in front of the class, taking part in discussions and performing in plays.

The best way to encourage speaking and listening skills at home is simply to talk to your child about the things that interest them. Miming games such as charades can also be good fun and help your child develop the confidence they need to role-play in class.

Reading

By the age of seven, children will be at different stages in their reading ability; some will be reading fluently, while others will still be learning. Children will continue to work with different methods of acquiring reading techniques, such as phonics and word recognition.

Children will also learn to read more critically, studying fiction and non-fiction books, and develop an understanding of techniques writers use. They'll look at the way a poet uses metaphor, for example, or the way a non-fiction writer uses particular words to persuade or explain.

They'll be studying a wide range of different texts – the literature they look at will include fiction (both contemporary and classic), poetry, myths and legends, and play scripts. Non-fiction texts they study will include newspapers, diaries, biographies and informational material, such as textbooks and reports.

At home, you can help by encouraging your child to read as much as possible – make regular visits to the library and, if you can, suggest different kinds of books, such as non-fiction or poetry. Of course, children often have very fixed ideas about what they like to read, so don't force it – almost any reading is better than none.

'To improve literacy, the best thing is to read a page every day. Some children are natural readers, but for children who aren't natural readers, a page a day makes a huge impact. Parents often finish the words for them if they're struggling. But let the child read it, and ask lots of questions about the page.'

Mr S, KS2 teacher.

Writing

In KS2, children will start learning about punctuation and grammar. They'll find out how to use punctuation marks such as full stops, commas, apostrophes and exclamation marks correctly, and also the meaning of words such as 'noun,' 'verb' and 'adjective'.

They'll build on the spelling they've already learnt and learn about spelling conventions (such as 'i before e'), patterns in spelling and how to check their spelling using a dictionary. They'll also learn a little about origins of words, common prefixes and suffixes and the use of terminology such as 'vowel' and 'consonant'.

Children are also expected to be using joined-up writing, and at some point will swap their pencils for a pen.

They will continue to write their own compositions, including stories, poems and non-fiction pieces, like reports, instructions and reviews. Learning to arrange material in a suitable way and write in a style appropriate for their audience is an important part of writing in KS2.

Some children love to write, while others find it a burden. Children who are good at expressing themselves creatively sometimes get taken to task for poor handwriting, which can deter them. Try to encourage your child's confidence in writing, perhaps by helping you make out a shopping list. You can also play games such as 'Boy, Girl, Animal, Vegetable' where you choose a letter of the alphabet and then every player has to write down a boy's name, girl's name, animal and vegetable beginning with that letter. It's a good way of developing both handwriting and spelling skills.

Mathematics

There are three broad topics covered by KS2 mathematics:

- Number and algebra.
- Space, shape and measures.
- Handling data.

The three topics are all connected, and teachers are expected to make sure that children understand the relationships between them.

As with literacy, the different elements of the mathematics curriculum are taught in blocks, which have to be taught in order. Each block is divided into units.

There's a big emphasis in the curriculum on equipping children with useful techniques for carrying out mathematical calculations. So while there's an element of repetition with the learning (mainly in learning the times tables), children also learn the strategies that can help them work out quite complicated sums.

Take a sum such as 66 x 5. Children will learn that you can work out this sum in different ways:

- Multiply 66 by 10, which gives you 660, and then divide by 2, which gives you 330.

- Multiply 60 by 5, which gives you 300, multiply 6 by 5, which gives you 30, and then add 300 and 30.

Another thread that runs through KS2 mathematics is communication. Children are expected to be able to present their findings coherently and to explain the reasoning by which they reached an answer.

'Times tables are really important – the foundation for everything. If a child has confidence in times tables, it has a huge impact.'

Mr S, KS2 teacher.

Number and algebra

Children learn in detail about the number system:

- How to use and apply number.

- How to perform calculations.

- How to solve numerical problems.

So they'll learn, for example, to count up in 10s or 100s from any two- or three-digit number (12, 22, 32 etc or 201, 301, 401).

By KS2, children usually know how to add and subtract, but now they'll learn to do multiplication and division. Division is usually taught using the 'bus stop' method, which looks like this:

$$8 \, \overline{\big)\, 360} \quad = 45$$

They'll begin learning their times tables, starting with the multiples of 2, 5 and 10, and will learn the techniques of long multiplication (such as 205 x 23).

They'll also learn about fractions, percentages and ratio, and understand the relationship between decimals and fractions (learning, for example, that 0.5 is the same as ½). They'll learn about how to round decimals up or down (rounding 1.9 up to 2, for example, or 3.1 down to 3).

There is also an element of mental maths. Tasks children are expected to perform mentally include:

■ Halve and double any two-digit number.

■ Add or subtract any pair of two-digit whole numbers (such as 45 – 23).

■ Multiply and divide numbers up to 100 (such as 27 x 3).

In KS2, children will also learn to use a calculator for more complicated calculations.

Space, shape and measures

Children are introduced to the principles of geometry – the properties of shapes and what happens when you manipulate them.

They learn to:

■ Use and apply shape, space and measures.

■ Understand properties of shape.

■ Understand properties of position and movement.

■ Understand measures.

They'll learn the importance of standard units of measurement and find out how to solve geometrical problems.

They will be learning to visualise 2D and 3D shapes (such as triangles and cubes) and to understand the properties of different shapes. They'll be expected to draw 2D and 3D shapes and to recognise their geometrical features, such as angles.

They'll also learn to recognise right angles, perpendicular and parallel lines, and to understand that angles are measured in degrees. Children will also learn to visualise and describe movement – to show that they know, for example, what happens if you rotate a triangle through 180 degrees.

Finally, they will learn about measures: to recognise the standard metric units (such as grams, litres and centimetres), to read scales and to calculate perimeters and areas of shapes. They'll also learn to tell the time, both from an analogue and digital clock.

Handling data

There are two components to this:

- Using and applying handling data.
- Processing, representing and interpreting data.

Data is important in other areas of the curriculum, particularly science. So a scientific experiment will often include comparing the weights or sizes of different items, or comparing the weight of an object before and after the experiment. The data-handling part of the mathematics curriculum enables children to develop those skills of gathering, recording and analysing data.

Children will learn to recognise the different ways data is represented (in tables and graphs, for example) and to interpret data presented in these ways. They'll learn to describe data sets using ideas such as 'mode' (as a measure of average) and to recognise different measures of probability i.e. how likely or unlikely something is to happen, given a particular set of information.

Here are some ways you can help your child develop mathematical skills:

'We as a cohort of parents were helped by an evening at the school teaching us maths methods nowadays in Key Stage 2. It helped parents realise it is all tricky and we now have much more patience with children.'

Catrin, mum of two.

- When you're cooking, ask your child to do the weighing and measuring – and ask how much of each ingredient you'd need if you were making twice as much.

- Introduce your child to maps, using a road atlas or map of your local area.

- On car journeys, use road signs displaying distance to practise addition and subtraction (e.g. 'If it's 30 miles to Reading, and 72 miles to London, how far is it from Reading to London?').

- In the shops, work out the relative prices of things. For example, if a 100g packet of biscuits costs 60p and a 150g packet costs 80p, which is better value?

Science

In KS2, there is a requirement to have two science lessons a week. There are four components to the science curriculum:

- Scientific enquiry.

- Life processes and living things.

- Materials and their properties.

- Physical processes.

As at KS1, the emphasis is on learning to think and act like a real scientist – to develop and test hypotheses, to gather evidence and make an impartial assessment of it, and to make further predictions based on the evidence.

The breadth of study (how children learn) for the science curriculum says that children will learn science through familiar domestic and environmental contexts (using a drum, for example, to learn about how sound is made, or growing flowers to understand about photosynthesis). They'll also learn to gather information from different sources, including ICT sources like the Internet.

Scientific enquiry

The skills of scientific enquiry are taught through the other three components which, as at KS1, map onto the traditional subjects of biology, chemistry and physics.

Scientific enquiry has two elements:

- Ideas and evidence in science.
- Investigative skills.

Children learn the importance of ideas and evidence in science – that it's a process of thinking creatively about explanations for how living and non-living things work, establishing links between causes and effect, and then testing those ideas using observation and evidence.

Jenner's vaccination work, for example, began with an observation that dairymaids who had suffered cowpox appeared immune from smallpox, and he hypothesised that one caused the other – an hypothesis that he then tested.

Children will develop their investigative skills through the stages of asking questions about what can be investigated scientifically and planning how they might find the answers; gathering and presenting evidence; and evaluating that evidence.

Life processes and living things

There are five components:

- Life processes.
- Humans and other animals.
- Green plants.
- Variation and classification.
- Living things in their environment.

Children learn the basics of biology: that certain processes (such as nutrition, growth and reproduction) are common to all living things; that the heart acts as a pump to circulate the blood through the body; what plants need to grow; how animals and plants can be classified into different groups; and how animals and plants are adapted to their habitat.

Materials and their properties

There are three components:

- Grouping and classifying materials.
- Changing materials.
- Separating mixtures of materials.

Children will learn about the different properties of materials and how this might make them suitable for use in particular situations. Some materials, for example, are better thermal insulators than others, while other materials are better electrical conductors. They'll also learn the differences between solids, liquids and gases.

They'll learn about what happens when materials are mixed (e.g. when you add salt to water) and to describe the changes that occur when materials, such as water or clay, are heated or cooled. They'll learn about the difference between reversible changes – cooling water so that it turns into ice, for example, and then heating it so it turns back into water – and irreversible changes, such as mixing two materials together to make something new, or burning a material like wood.

They'll learn techniques for separating mixtures of materials – such as using a sieve or a filter.

Physical processes

There are four components:

- Electricity.
- Forces and motion.
- Light and sound.
- The Earth and beyond.

Children build on what they learnt during KS1. So now, for example, they learn how to construct electrical circuits, incorporating a battery or power supply and a range of switches, to make electrical devices work. They'll learn how to represent circuits using drawings and symbols.

They'll also learn about different types of force (such as magnetic force, gravitational force and air resistance) and that when objects are pushed or pulled, an opposing push or pull can be felt.

They'll learn about the properties of light and sound: that light travels from a source and can be reflected from some surfaces, and sounds are made when objects vibrate, with the vibrations from a sound source requiring a medium (such as air or metal) to travel to the ear.

The earth and beyond is a new topic, introduced for the first time in KS2. Children learn about the orbits of the sun, earth and moon, and that day and night are related to the spin of the earth on its own axis.

Other subjects

As at KS1, teachers have greater freedom about how much time to devote to the foundation subjects (design and technology, ICT, history, geography, art and design, music and PE) and how to teach them than they do with the three core subjects. They may, for example, decide to take a whole week doing design and technology work to cover everything in that curriculum, rather than doing one lesson per week. The exception is PE, which has to be taught every week.

There are, nonetheless, certain topics and skills that children will be expected to learn. In history, for example, children will look at history from different perspectives – political, economic, technological and scientific. They will do this through studying several topics from British history (e.g. the Romans, Anglo-Saxons and Vikings, Tudor times, Victorian Britain, the Second World War), one topic from European history (e.g. the Ancient Greeks) and one topic from world history (e.g. Ancient Egypt).

Similarly, in geography children will learn geographical vocabulary and methods of geographical enquiry through studying two different localities: one in the UK and one in a country that is less economically developed. They will also study three themes: water and its effect on landscape and people; how settlements differ and change; and an environmental issue, such as traffic congestion.

Summing Up

- In KS2, your child will learn 11 subjects: the core subjects of mathematics, literacy and science, and eight foundation subjects.

- From September 2010, modern foreign languages will become a compulsory part of the KS2 curriculum.

- Each subject has a programme of study that outlines what children will learn in each subject.

- Teachers have to allocate fixed amounts of time to the teaching of maths, literacy and science, but they have more flexibility in how the other subjects are taught.

Chapter Nine

Key Stage 2 SATs

Taking SATs

Towards the end of Year 6, when your child is 11 or nearly 11, they will sit KS2 SATs in maths and literacy. The tests are given under exam conditions – that is, they are formal, strictly timed occasions and pupils will be aware that they are taking a test.

Once the tests have been completed, they are sent away to the QCDA for external marking. Schools receive the results in July.

What happens in the tests?

The tests will take place over a whole school week. In 2011, for the first time, the tests will be held in June (previously they were held in May).

There are seven tests:

- Reading test: 45 minutes, plus 15 minutes of reading time.
- Writing test (short): 20 minutes.
- Spelling test: 10 minutes.
- Writing test (long): 45 minutes.
- Mathematics Test A: 45 minutes.
- Mathematics Test B: 45 minutes.
- Mental mathematics test: 20 minutes.

At KS1, only more able pupils are given maths papers at level 3. At KS2, however, each paper includes questions from levels 3-5, so each pupil sits the same number of papers.

Contents of the tests

Reading test

Children are given a booklet to read on a particular topic, such as weather. The booklet will contain different kinds of writing – for example, a piece of fiction, a piece of non-fiction and a poem. They will also be given a booklet with about 30 questions about the passages they've read, to assess how much they've understood. The questions will vary in complexity; some will require short, one-word answers, while others will require several sentences.

Writing test (short)

Children are asked to produce one short piece of writing in 20 minutes. The writing could be fictional or non-fictional. In 2003, for example, they were asked to write a radio advertisement for a new toy. In 2007, they were given the first two sentences of a mystery story and asked to continue the beginning of the story.

Spelling test

The spelling test is given in the context of a piece of writing with blanks where 20 words are missing. When the teacher reads out the passage, pupils write the missing words in the blank spaces.

Writing test (long)

Children are asked to produce a longer piece of writing in 45 minutes, which includes 10 minutes of planning time. As with the shorter test, the writing may be fictional or non-fictional. The 2004 test, for example, asked pupils to write a speech giving their views on a new proposed school timetable. In 2007, they were asked to write a leaflet persuading friends and family to take care of the environment.

Mathematics Test A

This contains 20 to 25 questions mainly on arithmetic, with some simple geometry. Pupils are tested on addition, subtraction, multiplication, division, fractions and decimals. They are not allowed to use a calculator. Pupils are encouraged to show their working, so that even a wrong answer may get a point if the working shows the pupil has understood the principle.

Typical questions might be:

- Calculate $7.9 - 2.75$.

- Sweets cost 80p for 100 grams. What is the cost of 250 grams of sweets?

Mathematics Test B

This is similar to Mathematics Test A. Some of the questions are a little harder, and pupils are allowed to use a calculator. A typical question might be:

- Look at the sum:
  $73.4 + (88 \times 6.75)$
  Is the answer less than, equal to, or more than 1000?

Mental Mathematics Test

The teacher will read out 20 questions that children will be expected to work out in their head before writing down the answers. Typical questions might be:

- Divide eighty by four.

- What is fives times five added to six times three?

■ A carton of juice costs 75p. How many cartons of juice can you buy for £10?

Teacher assessment

As well as taking written tests, pupils are assessed by teachers in five areas:

■ Reading.

■ Writing.

■ Speaking and listening.

■ Maths.

■ Science.

Your child's final report from the school will give both the results of their SATs exam and their teacher assessment.

SATs scores

Parents will receive a report at the end of Year 6 giving their child's scores in each of the subjects covered in the SATs.

The vast majority of children will fall into levels 3, 4 or 5, though a small number of pupils with special educational needs will not reach level 3.

Most children are expected to achieve level 4 in each subject. A smaller number of more able children will achieve level 5, while lower achieving children may only achieve level 3.

Here are the national figures for 2009:

	Pupils at level 4	Pupils at level 5
Literacy (overall score that includes both reading and writing)	80%	29%
Reading	86%	47%
Writing	67%	19%
Mathematics	79%	35%

(Source: DfE, *National Curriculum Assessments at Key Stage 2 in England 2009.*)

Levels 4 and 5 are further subdivided into 'a', 'b' and 'c', where 'a' is the highest and 'c' is the lowest. Here is what the scores mean:

Score	Meaning
3	Achieving below the target for age 11.
4c	Working towards the expected standard for age 11.
4b	At the expected standard for age 11.
4a	Working easily within the expected standard, and nearly at the next stage.
5c	Working above the expected standard for age 11.
5b	Working well above the expected standard for age 11.
5a	Working well above the expected standard for age 11, and at the top end of the range for a Year 7 child.

How to prepare your child for SATs

We said in chapter 3 that SATs are not exams that your child can pass or fail, and that the aim of SATs is to assess the school's ability to teach its pupils, rather than to grade each child. This remains true of the KS2 SATs, but some secondary schools take both SATs results and teacher assessments into account when streaming children in Year 7.

As with KS1, you can buy practice tests online, but the chances are that your child will be doing lots of practice tests throughout Year 6, so there is arguably no additional value in doing extra ones at home. If your child enjoys using the computer, they may have fun playing some of the games on the BBC Bitesize website, which are tailored to the content of the National Curriculum.

Encourage your child as you always have done – by helping them find books that they enjoy reading and talking to your child about books they have read. Some children enjoy writing stories or keeping diaries or sending emails to friends – these are all good practice for writing. If you're worried about spelling, then you can try impromptu spelling tests ('I bet you can't spell "television"!') in the car or over breakfast. The same applies to maths – some children enjoy the challenge of occasional mental maths tests. Some examples:

- What's half of 56?
- What's 13 doubled?
- What's 8 x 7?

Summing Up

- Your child will sit SATs papers in literacy and maths near the end of Year 6.

- The papers are marked by external examiners.

- Your child will also receive a teacher assessment in literacy, maths and science.

- SATs scores are represented as levels (3, 4a, 4b, 4c and 5a, 5b and 5c). The expected standard for this age is 4b.

Help List

Advisory Centre for Education

1c Aberdeen Studios, 22 Highbury Grove, London, N5 2DQ
Tel: 0808 800 5793 (helpline)
www.ace-ed.org.uk
Provides information about state education in England and Wales for 5-16-year olds, with telephone advice on educational issues such as exclusions, admissions and special educational needs matters.

BBC Bitesize KS1 resources

www.bbc.co.uk/schools/ks1bitesize
Learning resources for KS1 pupils.

BBC Bitesize KS2 resources

www.bbc.co.uk/schools/ks2bitesize
Learning resources for KS2 pupils.

BBC Learning: Parents

www.bbc.co.uk/schools/parents
Advice on schools for parents.

BBC Parenting

www.bbc.co.uk/parenting
Website dedicated to parenting with lots of information on pre-school- and primary school-aged children.

BBC Schools

www.bbc.co.uk/schools
Website dedicated to schools with lots of information for parents on how to help your child at home and at school.

British Dyslexia Association

Unit 8, Bracknell Beeches, Old Bracknell Lane, Bracknell, RG12 7BW
Tel: 0845 251 9002
www.bdadyslexia.org.uk
Aims to advance education and employment opportunities for people with
dyslexia. A wide list of books, brochures and software is available.

Cbeebies

www.bbc.co.uk/cbeebies
Website containing fun games to play with children during foundation stage
(0-5 years old). There is also information for parents, including articles on how
children learn and special educational needs.

Crickweb

www.crickweb.co.uk
Free interactive resources and activities for foundation stage, KS1 and KS2.

Department for Education (DfE)

www.education.gov.uk
Government department with responsibility for children, families and
education. You can view league tables by clicking on 'school performance
tables' at the bottom of the home page.

Directgov

www.direct.gov.uk
Official government advice site. Click on 'parents' for information about
schools, learning and development. There is also information on becoming a
school governor.

Dyscalculia Centre

www.dyscalculia.me.uk
Resources for parents and teachers for children with dyscalculia (a condition
that hinders children's ability to develop arithmetical skills).

Dyspraxia Foundation

8 West Alley, Hitchin, Herts, SG5 1EG
Tel: 01462 454 986 (helpline, Monday to Friday, 10am-1pm)
dyspraxia@dyspraxiafoundation.org.uk
www.dyspraxiafoundation.org.uk
Charity committed to making the teaching and medical professions more aware of dyspraxia, and to spread understanding of how those who have the condition can be helped.

Emaths

www.emaths.co.uk
Maths resources website. Past SATs papers for KS1 and KS2 can be found by clicking on 'learn'.

Good Schools Guide

www.goodschoolsguide.co.uk
A guide to both independent and state schools.

Independent Schools Inspectorate (ISI)

CAP House, 9-12 Long Lane, London, EC1A 9HA
Tel: 020 7600 0100
www.isi.net
Approved body for inspecting independent schools. On the website, you can access reports on ISI inspections since 2000.

Learning and Teaching Scotland

www.ltscotland.org.uk
Information on the new Scottish Curriculum for Excellence can be found on this website.

National Confederation of Parent Teachers Associations

www.ncpta.org.uk
Charity representing PTAs in England, Wales and Northern Ireland.

National Curriculum

http://curriculum.qcda.gov.uk
Information on the National Curriculum in England. The site is mainly for schools but the information is useful for parents too.

National Governors' Association

www.nga.org.uk
Website of the body representing school governors in England.

National Strategies

http://nationalstrategies.standards.dcsf.gov.uk
Information on the government strategies regarding the EYFS and primary school stages.

Northern Ireland Curriculum

www.nicurriculum.org.uk
Information on the Northern Ireland Curriculum.

Office of the Schools Adjudicator

Mowden Hall, Staindrop Road, Darlington, DL3 9BG
Tel: 0870 0012468
OSA.TEAM@osa.gsi.gov.uk
www.schoolsadjudicator.gov.uk
A body set up by the government to adjudicate in disputes about admissions. The school adjudicators will not look at cases involving individual children, just at whether the admissions rules themselves are fair.

Ofsted

Royal Exchange Buildings, St Ann's Square, Manchester, M2 7LA
enquiries@ofsted.gov.uk
www.ofsted.gov.uk
The body responsible for inspecting and regulating schools. Click on 'inspection reports' to view reports on schools throughout the UK.

Qualifications and Curriculum Development Agency (QCDA)

53-55 Butts Road, Earlsdon Park, Coventry, CV1 3BH
info@qcda.gov.uk
www.qcda.gov.uk
The body responsible for developing the National Curriculum, improving and delivering assessments, and reviewing and reforming qualifications.

School Appeals

www.schoolappeals.org.uk
Independent website offering advice on school appeals.

Schoolsnet

www.schoolsnet.com
A guide to UK schools, written by parents.

The School Gate

www.bbc.co.uk/wales/schoolgate
A BBC resource for parents in Wales. There is information on the Welsh curriculum and how to help your child learn.

Times SchoolGate blog

http://timesonline.typepad.com/schoolgate
Useful blog discussing a wide variety of educational issues, aimed at parents, teachers and students.

Times Educational Supplement

www.tes.co.uk
Website of the weekly newspaper for teachers

Welsh Assembly Government

www.wales.gov.uk
The official site of the Welsh Assembly Government. Click on 'education and skills' for information on the Welsh curriculum.

Book List

A Guide for Parents – At home with the Oxford Reading Tree
By Oxford University Press, Oxford.

Early Years Foundation Stage Profile – Assessment Scales Reference Sheet
By QCDA, London, 2008.

I am Too Absolutely Small for School
By Lauren Child, Orchard Books, London, 2010.

Independent Review of the Primary Curriculum: Final Report
By Sir Jim Rose, DCSF, London, 2009.

It's Child's Play – Early Years Foundation Stage
By DCSF, London, 2008.

Jolly Phonics Workbooks
By Susan M Lloyd, Jolly Learning Ltd, Essex, 1995.

Kevin Goes to School
By Liesbet Slegers, Frances Lincoln Publishers, London, 2005.

School Admissions Code
By DCSF, London, 2009.
(Available for free from www.dcsf.gov.uk/sacode/downloads/
SchoolAdmissionsCodeWEB060309.pdf)

Starting School
By Alan & Janet Ahlberg, Puffin Books, London, 1990.

Superphonics Spelling
By Ruth Miskin, Hodder Children's Books, London, 2008.

Topsy and Tim Start School
By Jean & Gareth Adamson, Ladybird Books, London, 2009.

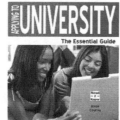